Christopher B. Barry
Texas Christian University

John W. Peavy III, CFA
Founders Trust Company

Mauricio Rodriguez
Texas Christian University

Emerging Stock Markets:
Risk, Return, and Performance

The Research Foundation of
The Institute of Chartered Financial Analysts

Research Foundation Publications

Emerging Stock Markets:
Risk, Return, and Performance

This publication is designed to provide accurate and authoritative information in regard to the subject matter covered. It is sold with the understanding that the publisher is not engaged in rendering legal, accounting, or other professional service. If legal advice or other expert assistance is required, the services of a competent professional should be sought.

The Institute of Chartered Financial Analysts is a subsidiary of the Association for Investment Management and Research.

ISBN-0-943205-45-X

Printed in the United States of America

June 1997

Editorial Staff

Bette Collins
Editor

Roger Mitchell
Assistant Editor

Jaynee M. Dudley
Production Manager

Christine P. Martin
Production Coordinator

Diane B. Hamshar
Typesetting/Layout

Mission

$\mathcal{T}$he Research Foundation's mission is to identify, fund, and publish research that is relevant to the AIMR Global Body of Knowledge and useful for AIMR member investment practitioners and investors.

The Research Foundation of
The Institute of Chartered Financial Analysts
P.O. Box 3668
Charlottesville, Virginia 22903
U.S.A.
Telephone: 804-980-3655
Fax: 804-963-6826
E-mail: rf@aimr.org
http://www.aimr.org/aimr/research/research.html

Biographies of Authors

Christopher B. Barry is a professor of finance and holds the Robert and Maria Lowdon Chair of Business Administration in the M.J. Neeley School of Business at Texas Christian University. Previously, he served as chair of the Department of Finance at Southern Methodist University and held positions on the faculties of The University of Texas at Austin and the University of Florida. Professor Barry also has taught extensively throughout Latin America and Europe. He is the author of numerous journal articles in the areas of uncertainty in portfolio management and capital markets, the going-public process, venture capital, and emerging capital markets. Professor Barry is book review editor of the *Journal of Finance* and associate editor of the *Journal of Investing, Emerging Markets Quarterly*, and the *Latin American Business Review*. He holds a B.S. from Georgia Tech and a D.B.A. from Indiana University.

John W. Peavy III, CFA, is chair of the board and chief investment officer of Founders Trust Company. He also serves as adjunct professor of finance at the American Graduate School of International Management (Thunderbird) and as an instructor in the Personal Trust Administration School of the Texas Bankers Association and the Graduate Finance Certificate program at Southern Methodist University. Previously, Mr. Peavy served as the Mary Jo Vaughn-Rauscher Chair of Financial Investments and chair of the Department of Finance in the Edwin L. Cox School of Business at Southern Methodist University and was the Arthur J. Morris Visiting Professor of Finance at the Colgate Darden Graduate School of Business at the University of Virginia. He is associate editor of the *Journal of Investing* and serves on the editorial boards of the *Financial Analysts Journal* and the *Review of Financial Economics*. Mr. Peavy is the author of four books and numerous articles published in leading academic and professional journals and writes *The Peavy Point of View* newsletter. He holds a B.B.A. from Southern Methodist University, an M.B.A. from the Wharton School at the University of Pennsylvania, and a Ph.D. from The University of Texas at Arlington.

Mauricio Rodriguez is an assistant professor of finance in the M.J. Neeley School of Business at Texas Christian University. He is the author of articles published in finance and real estate academic journals. Professor Rodriguez is an associate editor of the *Journal of Real Estate* Literature and a member of the board of directors of the International Real Estate Society. He holds a B.B.A. from The George Washington University, an M.B.A. from The American University, and a Ph.D. from the University of Connecticut.

Contents

Foreword

There is an old joke that goes something like this: Late one night, a man is on his hands and knees under a lamppost, obviously searching for something. A passerby stops and asks the man what he is looking for. "My keys," responds the man. "Where exactly did you lose them?" the other asks. "About half a block down on the other side of the street." "Why are you looking here then?" "Because the light is better," he replies.

Unfortunately, this story can serve as a metaphor for some of the empirical research conducted by financial economists today. Too often, researchers are forced away from tackling the most interesting conceptual questions on a particular topic because of various inadequacies in the data required to answer them. An excellent example is the study of security performance in a country with an emerging market. For several years, investors and researchers have been intrigued with the promise of these stocks but have been frustrated in their efforts to find the information they need to perform the requisite analyses. Indeed, even the data that did exist were frequently incomplete, unreliable, and hard to compare across borders.

In this monograph, Christopher Barry, John Peavy, and Mauricio Rodriguez allay this frustration by shining a light directly on the keys to understanding how emerging markets have functioned in the past two decades. Their work makes two contributions. First, and quite possibly foremost, the authors have done a thorough (and, by their own admission, painstaking) job of analyzing and summarizing stock return data for more than two dozen countries in the Emerging Markets Data Base maintained by the International Finance Corporation at the World Bank. The country-specific historical return and risk series they report—as well as the statistics for aggregate and regional indexes of these countries—offer readers a remarkable snapshot of the evolution in the investment performance, on both a local currency and U.S. dollar basis, of the emerging sector of the global economy. Simply stated, no other compendium of this information is currently available.

Although refining a database that will keep researchers busy for years to come would be enough of an accomplishment for many authors, Barry, Peavy, and Rodriguez do not stop there. Their second achievement is to scrutinize these return series to confirm or refute some of the most widely held beliefs about the way emerging markets operate. Their findings are enlightening—and sometimes surprising. For instance, the risk–reward trade-off in many of these developing countries has changed dramatically over time and in a way that contradicts the usual time diversification arguments advanced in many textbooks. The authors confirm the relatively low correlation coefficients between emerging and developed market securities (hence, the diversification benefits of including the former in portfolios of the latter) but caution that these correlations are extremely volatile when measured historically. To many readers, these results will go a long way toward establishing the efficacy of emerging market investments as a separate asset class.

One cannot describe the potential impact of this monograph without mentioning Roger Ibbotson and Rex Sinquefield's *Stocks, Bonds, Bills, and Inflation* (*SBBI*), an ongoing project that was first published by the Research Foundation of the Institute of Chartered Financial Analysts almost a decade ago. In that work, Ibbotson and

Sinquefield provided return data and asset classifications for capital markets in the United States for the majority of the 20th century. So pervasive is *SBBI*'s impact that few investment practitioners are untouched by its influence; it is truly *the* definitive support reference for research on topics in the U.S. market ranging from security evaluation to performance measurement. Ten years from now, *Emerging Stock Markets: Risk, Return, and Performance*, which is loosely patterned after *SBBI*, could well be described in the same terms for this increasingly important set of securities.

With this volume, Barry, Peavy, and Rodriguez push the frontier of research into emerging stock markets farther than it has ever been before. Without question, no extant source contains such a complete "A to Z" coverage of the topic, and for this effort, they are to be commended. As impressive as this work is, however, I suspect that the ultimate legacy of the research that you are now holding will be the future projects it inspires; this monograph will shine a light in the right direction for years to come. The Research Foundation is pleased to bring it to your attention.

Keith C. Brown, CFA
Research Director
The Research Foundation of the
Institute of Chartered Financial Analysts

Acknowledgments

We appreciate the assistance provided by Rufat Alimardanov, Sean Conner, Shane Evatt, Deron Kawamoto, Francisco Lorenzo, Duane McPherson, Lee Neathery, Federico Ochoa, John Olsen, and Judi Wilson. Any errors are, of course, the responsibility of the authors. We would also like to thank the International Finance Corporation for making their Emerging Markets Data Base available to us for this endeavor. Finally, we would like to thank the Research Foundation of the Institute of Chartered Financial Analysts and AIMR for their support.

Christopher B. Barry
John W. Peavy III, CFA
Mauricio Rodriguez

Introduction

The primary objective of this monograph is to provide a comprehensive source of historical data about the performance of securities in emerging markets. Although historical returns cannot be relied on to predict future performance, such empirical data can provide useful insights for financial and investment managers. A wide array of informational sources report historical security returns in developed countries, but only recently have investors and managers had access to data about returns of stocks in emerging markets.

Another objective of the monograph is to reveal important historical trade-offs between risk and return and to demonstrate how risk–return relationships vary over time. We also illustrate the effects on risk and return of adding emerging market securities to traditional U.S. stock portfolios. Our overall intent is to provide a comprehensive knowledge base that will enable the investor or investment manager to make informed investment decisions regarding emerging market assets.

What Are Emerging Markets?

Although the term "emerging markets" was introduced only recently, such markets have long been a recognized investment alternative among institutional and individual investors. Indeed, many of the world's most successful investors have accepted the emerging markets as a separate asset class.

Unfortunately, no universally accepted definition of an emerging market exists, nor does a consensus about which markets merit the "emerging" status. In the 1960s, Japan was an emerging market, and only slightly more than a century has passed since the United States was considered to be an emerging market. In short, the composition of the emerging market universe is in a continual state of flux. Today's emerging market may be tomorrow's vibrant economy—thus, the attractiveness and excitement of this important asset class.

The World Bank, by far the largest investor in these markets, defines a "developing" country as one having a per capita gross national product of less than US$8,626 (IFC 1995a). According to this definition, 170 economies fall into the developing category. Only a handful of the many countries that can be called developing merit the emerging title, however. "Emerging" implies the kind of growth and change that lead to investment opportunities—growth and change that can occur only as the people of a country gain realistic possibilities for improved economic, social, and political conditions. Investors strive to identify the emerging markets among the developing countries and invest in those markets, but they tend to shun the markets that do not possess the important traits that classify them as emerging.

To attract the attention and capital of foreign investors, an emerging market must also be investable. Although developing countries contain approximately 85 percent of the world's population, they represent only about 13 percent of the world's stock market capitalization. This disproportionate population-to-capitalization mix vividly indicates the future growth potential for stocks in developing countries, but it also indicates the selectivity that must accompany investments in these markets. The

International Finance Corporation (IFC), a leading compiler of emerging market returns, considers the size (as measured by market capitalization) and liquidity (as measured by turnover) of a market in classifying that market as emerging and in deciding to commence coverage of the market and to include the securities in the market in its Emerging Markets Data Base (EMDB). In addition, inclusion in the EMDB is affected by the industry in which a company operates; the IFC attempts to provide broad coverage of industries important within the market. Thus, a smaller, less liquid security might be included whereas a larger, more liquid one is excluded if the former security represents a particular industry, which would otherwise be underrepresented.

Currently, the IFC includes the stocks of 26 countries in the EMDB and includes 25 of those country markets in its *investable* index. (Nigeria is considered not investable because the market is closed to foreign investors.) Four of those countries—Korea, Malaysia, South Africa, and Taiwan—account for approximately 50 percent of the weighting of the market capitalization of the investable index. So, an investor might question the diversification benefits of such a concentrated grouping.

Significant differences exist among emerging markets, but as a group, they share one primary similarity—change. Through improved communications, individuals all over the world can see the rewards of economic growth, and they want to participate. The rising aspirations of people and demographic realities are driving changes in developing countries. When development and political reform give rise to structural changes, economic growth and the rewards associated with it persist. The economic growth, in turn, leads to profitable opportunities for investors. Of course, risks accompany these emerging market opportunities. Investors can foster success, however, by seeking out economies that have or will soon have political stability, open markets, policies that encourage growth, strong institutional structures, clearly defined investment rules, equitable taxation, market liquidity, and satisfactory intermediaries.

The Appeal of Emerging Market Investing

The primary motivation of investors in emerging markets is the desire to add value at the margin to a conventional world or domestic portfolio for some period. Emerging market equities may be one of the smallest asset groups in terms of current value of market capitalization, but they constitute potentially the fastest growing investment class. At year-end 1975, the total market capitalization of emerging markets was substantially less than the market value of IBM Corporation alone. By 1985, however, the markets had grown dramatically, and as Table 1 shows, the market capitalization of stocks in emerging markets increased from US$167.7 billion in 1985 to about US$1.8 trillion in 1995, a more than 10-fold increase. In this same time period, the stock market capitalization of developed countries only approximately tripled—from US$4.5 trillion in 1985 to US$15.9 trillion in 1995. Consequently, emerging market stocks climbed from a 3.6 percent share of world market capitalization in 1985 to an 11.9 percent share in 1995.

The dramatic growth in the market value of emerging market stocks is attributable to three factors. The most important growth factor is the appreciation over time of the individual securities composing these markets. The second factor is the inclusion of new countries in the emerging market group. After 1985, eight new countries were added to the group. Finally, value growth occurred as new stocks

Table 1. Market Capitalization of Emerging Markets, 1985–95
(US$ millions)

Market (Month/Year[a])	1985	1986	1987	1988	1989	1990	1991	1992	1993	1994	1995
Argentina (12/75)	2,037	1,591	1,519	2,025	4,225	3,268	18,509	18,633	43,967	36,864	37,783
Brazil (12/75)	42,768	42,096	16,900	32,149	44,368	16,354	42,759	45,261	99,430	189,281	147,636
Chile (12/75)	2012	4,062	5,341	6,849	9,587	13,645	27,984	29,644	44,622	68,195	73,860
China (12/92)	—	—	—	—	—	—	2,028	18,255	40,567	43,521	42,055
Colombia (12/84)	416	822	1,255	1,145	1,136	1,416	4,036	5,681	9,237	14,028	17,893
Greece (12/75)	765	1,129	4,464	4,285	6,376	15,228	13,118	9,489	12,319	14,921	17,060
Hungary (12/92)	—	—	—	—	—	—	505	562	812	1,604	2,399
India (12/75)	14,364	13,588	17,057	23,623	27,316	38,567	47,730	65,119	97,976	127,515	127,199
Indonesia (12/89)	117	81	68	253	2,254	8,081	6,823	12,038	32,953	47,241	66,585
Jordan (1/78)	2,454	2,839	2,643	2,233	2,162	2,001	2,512	3,365	4,891	4,594	4,670
Korea (12/75)	7,381	13,924	32,905	94,238	140,946	110,594	96,373	107,448	139,420	191,778	181,955
Malaysia (12/84)	16,229	15,065	18,531	23,318	39,842	48,611	58,627	94,004	220,328	199,276	222,729
Mexico (12/75)	3,815	5,952	8,371	13,784	22,550	32,725	98,178	139,061	200,671	130,246	90,694
Nigeria (12/84)	2,743	1,112	974	960	1,005	1,372	1,882	1,221	1,029	2,711	2,033
Pakistan (12/84)	1,370	1,710	1,960	2,460	2,457	2,850	7,326	8,028	11,602	12,263	9,286
Peru (12/92)	760	2,322	831	—	931	812	1,118	2,630	5,113	8,178	11,795
Philippines (12/84)	669	2,008	2,948	4,280	11,965	5,927	10,197	13,794	40,327	55,519	58,859
Poland (12/92)	—	—	—	—	—	—	144	222	2,706	3,057	4,564
Portugal (1/86)	192	1,530	8,857	7,172	10,618	9,201	9,613	9,213	12,417	16,249	18,362
South Africa (1/94)	55,439	102,652	128,663	126,094	131,060	137,540	168,497	103,537	171,942	225,718	280,526
Sri Lanka (12/92)	365	421	608	471	427	917	1,936	1,439	2,498	2,884	1,998
Taiwan (12/84)	10,432	15,367	48,634	120,017	237,012	100,710	124,864	101,124	195,198	247,325	187,206
Thailand (12/75)	1,856	2,878	5,485	8,811	25,648	23,896	35,815	58,259	130,510	131,479	141,507
Turkey (12/86)	—	935	3,221	1,135	6,783	19,065	15,703	9,931	37,496	21,605	20,772
Venezuela (12/84)	1,128	1,510	2,278	1,816	1,472	8,361	11,214	7,600	8,010	4,111	3,655
Zimbabwe (12/75)	360	410	718	774	1,067	2,395	1,394	628	1,433	1,828	2,038
Total	167,672	234,004	314,231	477,892	731,207	603,536	808,885	866,186	1,567,474	1,801,991	1,775,119

[a]The date in parentheses denotes when IFC coverage began.

became publicly available in the emerging countries. For example, some US$13 billion of the increased market capitalization of the Argentine Bolsa was accounted for by the privatization (and public offering of shares) of YPF (the former national oil and gas company) and two telecommunications firms. Overall, the number of companies in the emerging markets covered by the EMDB more than doubled from 1985 to 1995, going from 8,207 to 16,751. In comparison, the number of investable companies in U.S. markets increased only 7.4 percent in this time period.

Emerging markets have become increasingly attractive to investors as the developing countries focus on creating favorable conditions for economic growth. The low correlations of emerging markets with each other and, as a group, with developed markets combined with the emerging markets' growth prospects provide the potential for enhancing the return and reducing the risk of the total portfolio.

Many prospective investors in emerging markets proceed with caution, however; they recognize that the risks must be carefully evaluated and understood. Emerging market investors must cope with high market volatility, economic and political instability, dramatic currency swings, illiquidity, high transaction costs, rapid but volatile growth, constant change, and a limited amount of reliable information. For such reasons, most investors find that investing in only one or a few emerging markets is an excessively risky approach. Annual standard deviations of returns may exceed 50 percent, which is high enough to cause even the most venturesome investor to pause. The risks can be illustrated by Argentina's market in 1991 and 1992: In 1991, Argentina adopted a currency plan that made the Argentine currency convertible with the U.S. dollar. In that year, the Argentine Bolsa registered a dollar-denominated return of almost 400 percent. Many investors were attracted to the market, and the market rose an additional 38 percent early in 1992. Then, from May through November of 1992, the market lost more than 56 percent of its value.

Selection of Emerging Markets for the Study

Because the focus of this study is on investment rates of return and risk, the study uses the IFC's classification scheme of a subset of developing economies that are deemed to be emerging markets. As the viability of emerging markets has increased, so has the IFC's coverage. Thus, the current IFC emerging market universe provides a representative cross-section of emerging economies.

The IFC's EMDB has gained recognition as one of the world's premier sources for reliable, comprehensive information and statistics on stock markets in developing countries. At this point in time, the EMDB covers the 26 markets examined in this study with information collected since 1975 and provides regular updates on the more than 1,600 stocks in its composite index. EMDB data do contain a "look-back" bias; stocks existing as of 1981 were tracked back to 1975 in some instances.

EMDB products are available in computerized form and as publications. Three levels of computerized data can be provided: comprehensive data on individual stocks covered in all markets, data series for each index computed, and data series for each market covered.

The IFC began to produce its own standardized stock indexes for developing countries in mid-1981. Using a sample of stocks in each market, the IFC calculates indexes of stock market performance designed to serve as benchmarks calculated on a consistent basis across national boundaries. These indexes eliminate the difficulties in comparing markets that arise from inconsistencies among locally produced indexes with differing methodologies.

The original IFC indexes were calculated only once a year, used end-month prices, were based on the 10–20 most active stocks in each of 10 emerging markets, were equally weighted, and were available on a "price only" and total returns basis. Nine of the 10 markets had a history back to December 1975; one (Jordan) had a base in January 1978, when the Amman Financial Market first opened. Gradually, calculation periods tightened up to once a quarter, on end-month prices. The IFC now provides monthly indexes from the end of 1975 for nine markets and weekly indexes for several markets from the end of 1988.

The IFC's composite index combines country market indexes and thus can serve as a measure of return and diversification benefits from broad-based emerging market investing.

In late 1985, the IFC changed its methodology from equal weighting to market-capitalization weighting, improved the timeliness of calculation of end-month indexes from a quarterly to a one-month lag, expanded the number of stocks covered, and increased the number of markets covered from 10 to 17. In addition, the IFC added regional indexes for Latin America and Asia to supplement the all-market composite index.

The new IFC indexes, with a base date of December 1984, were launched in January 1987 and proved to be very popular with money managers. Other markets were added to coverage in 1989 (Portugal and Turkey, with base periods back to 1986) and in 1990 (Indonesia, with a base period of December 1989). Beginning in 1988, the IFC improved the timeliness of index calculation from end month, with considerable lag, to end week with a one-week lag.

From 1988 until 1992, the IFC expanded the number of stocks covered in the indexes and added to the number of data variables available for each stock. In mid-1991, the IFC released the industry indexes, which sorted the stocks of the IFC Composite Index by industry categories.

The IFC introduced investable indexes in March 1993. Adjusted to reflect the accessibility of markets and individual stocks to foreign investors, the IFC investable indexes offer a performance benchmark for international investors who might view the illiquid or restricted securities in a market to be irrelevant. The former series of IFC indexes were renamed the "global indexes" to distinguish them from the new series.

In 1993, the IFC launched indexes for China, Hungary, Peru, Poland, and Sri Lanka. South Africa was added in 1994, and the Czech Republic in 1995.

Table 2 shows the wide variations among the year-end stock market capitalizations of the emerging markets. For example, at year-end 1995, South Africa's market capitalization of US$280.5 billion was more than 140 times Sri Lanka's at US$1.9 billion. Table 3 shows the impact of the market capitalizations on the market weightings in the IFC indexes.

Construction of the Study Indexes and Calculation of Returns

For this study, we constructed indexes using EMDB data back to December 31, 1975. The first period is the 9 1/2-year period from the start of the sample, January 1976, through June 1985; the second period is the subsequent 10 years, July 1985 through June 1995. For simplicity, we will be referring to 20-, 10-, and 5-year periods when discussing results. We developed indexes by country or regional market and for a composite. We calculated those returns (given in the appendix) after adjusting the EMDB data for certain timing problems in the reporting of some information and then constructed indexes based on those adjusted returns.

Table 2. Stock Market Capitalization, December 31, 1995

(US$ billions)

Country	Market Capitalization	Country	Market Capitalization
South Africa	280.5	Turkey	20.7
Malaysia	222.7	Portugal	18.3
Taiwan	187.2	Colombia	17.8
Korea	181.9	Greece	17.0
Brazil	147.6	Peru	11.7
Thailand	141.5	Pakistan	9.2
India	127.1	Jordan	4.6
Mexico	90.6	Poland	4.5
Chile	73.8	Venezuela	3.6
Indonesia	66.5	Hungary	2.3
Philippines	58.8	Nigeria	2.0
China	42.0	Zimbabwe	2.0
Argentina	37.7	Sri Lanka	1.9

Individual local returns were calculated for each company that had data available from the IFC. Similar to firm returns found in the Center for Research in Security Prices (CRSP) files, we adjusted prices for return calculations to reflect stock splits, stock dividends, new issues, and rights issues. The reported return series includes dividends paid during the return period. The individual stock return calculation for month t can be expressed as follows:

$$R_{it} = \frac{S_t P_t[1 - (RIS_t SP_t) / (S_{t-1} PRIS_t + RIS_t SP_t)] + D_t S_t - P_t S_{new}}{S_t P_{t-1}} - 1,$$

where:

S_t = number of shares outstanding at time t (including new shares from stock splits and stock dividends)

P_t = price per share at time t

RIS_t = number of new shares from rights issues during period t

SP_t = subscription price for the rights issue

$PRIS_t$ = pre-rights-issue price per share at time t

S_{new} = number of other new shares issued during period t

D_t = cash dividends paid during period t

Because subscription prices for new issues were not available, the current value associated with new issues was subtracted out of the return calculation.

In several cases, the IFC recorded dividend, stock split, or rights issue information at a date later than the actual date, perhaps because of late notification to the IFC. We aligned all of the data so that all information of this nature was dated back to the date on which the event occurred. Dollar-based returns were calculated from exchange rate information available in the IFC data files.

The indexes for the study are based on value-weighted portfolios for each market. Value-weighted return series were also calculated for the regional portfolios and the composite portfolio. The value-weighted return for a given market portfolio was calculated as the weighted average of the returns of the individual stocks in the portfolio as follows:

$$R_{pt} = \sum_{i=1}^{N} W_{i,\,t-1} r_{it} \, ,$$

where $W_{i,t-1}$ is the market value weight of security i at the end of period t–1.

Similarly to how CRSP value-weighted portfolio returns and other common value-weighted return series are calculated, the weight assigned to a security's return for this study is its percentage of total market capitalization from the end of the previous period. Given that new companies appeared (and some disappeared) as the emerging markets grew, the number of firms in a given market portfolio is not constant. The number of firms in a portfolio at a given point in time depends on the number of firms with valid returns.

The process of calculating individual rate-of-return data and then computing value-weighted returns resulted in market returns very much like those reported for the IFC Global Index. Our value-weighted portfolio returns for individual emerging markets were highly correlated with IFC Global-Index-based returns (an R^2 of more than 90 percent).

Table 3. Market Weights in the IFC Indexes, End of March 1995

Market	Total Market Capitalization (US$ millions)	IFC Global Index			IFC Investable Index		
		Number of Stocks	Market Capitalization (US$ millions)	Weight in IFC Composite	Number of Stocks	Market Capitalization (US$ millions)	Weight in IFC Composite
IFC regional indexes							
Composite	1,431,782	1,590	1,084,602	100.0	1,136	605,551	100.0
Latin America	371,521	325	244,054	22.5	251	169,341	28.0
Asia	995,326	933	633,897	58.4	677	238,808	39.4
Europe/Mideast/ Africa	64,935	332	206,650	19.1	208	197,402	32.6
Europe/Mideast/Africa							
Greece	17,060	50	10,161	0.9	40	9,638	1.6
Jordan	4,670	50	3,484	0.3	8	1,116	0.2
Nigeria	2,033	35	1,537	0.1	—	0	—
Portugal	18,362	30	10,932	1.0	26	8,627	1.4
Turkey	20,772	44	13,782	1.3	44	13,782	2.3
Zimbabwe	2,038	24	1,517	0.1	5	179	0.0
Latin America							
Argentina	37,783	34	22,148	2.0	30	22,015	3.6
Brazil	147,636	87	94,615	8.7	71	63,329	10.5
Chile	73,860	47	48,070	4.4	16	11,229	1.9
Colombia	17,893	25	8,519	0.8	16	8,111	1.3
Mexico	90,694	80	60,866	5.6	67	55,479	9.2
Venezuela	3,655	16	2,483	0.2	12	2,356	0.4
East Asia							
Philippines	58,859	45	31,965	2.9	25	16,950	2.8
South Korea	181,955	162	123,648	2.3	159	17,112	2.8
Taiwan	187,206	93	113,032	10.4	93	16,955	2.8
South Asia							
India	127,199	123	57,753	5.3	101	13,489	2.2
Indonesia	66,585	50	37,703	3.5	42	19,631	3.2
Malaysia	222,729	114	142,494	13.1	114	118,996	19.7
Pakistan	9,286	80	6,482	0.6	36	4,832	0.8
Thailand	141,507	76	94,963	8.8	68	28,176	4.7

Structure of the Monograph

This monograph begins with a presentation and discussion of historical rates of return for stocks in 26 emerging country markets, for a composite index of emerging market stocks, and for subindexes of broad geographical regions. The monthly returns are in the appendix. For comparison purposes, we have included return data for U.S. stocks, U.S. Treasury bills, and U.S. domestic inflation.[1] These additional data allow the reader to explore fundamental real-versus-nominal and risk-versus-return relationships. Standard deviations were computed for the individual emerging markets, for the composite index, and for regional indexes. Standard deviations for domestic stocks, U.S. T-bills, and inflation were calculated and included for comparison purposes.

Chapter 1 provides the investor with comprehensive data about the rates of return and risk of emerging markets in the aggregate, for selected regions, and for individual countries. Returns are presented in U.S. dollar terms and in terms of local currencies. This information is designed to equip the investor with solid empirical data documenting the historical performance of securities in emerging markets. A particular focus of Chapter 1 is changes in emerging market returns over time.

Because one of the purported benefits of emerging market securities is their low correlations among themselves (across markets, although not within markets) and with securities in developed markets, Chapter 2 addresses portfolio combinations of emerging market assets with U.S. domestic securities. The chapter deals explicitly with empirical results needed for portfolio construction. We present comprehensive statistical information showing the correlations between the various emerging markets and the U.S. market (and between the emerging markets) and discuss how securities from all of these markets can be combined to form efficient portfolios.

Chapter 3 compares the performance of the full set of EMDB markets with an investable subset of the EMDB universe. The chapter then goes on to discuss the effect of using the investable subset only in portfolios of U.S. stocks.

Chapter 4 of the monograph analyzes the performance of country, regional, and broad-based closed-end emerging market funds. This final chapter focuses on the pros and cons of achieving exposure to the emerging markets through such funds.

---

[1]Based on Ibbotson Associates data.

1. Historical Performance of Emerging Equity Markets

A key consequence of the relative newness of emerging markets as an investable outlet is the limited information on historical rates of return for securities in these markets. Investors in securities of developed markets have access to extensive historical performance results for long periods of time. Unfortunately, performance results for emerging markets do not exist for such extended time periods. Although securities have existed and traded in emerging markets for many decades, reliable performance results exist for a much briefer time. The International Finance Corporation's (IFC's) Emerging Markets Data Base (EMDB) dates back only to year-end 1975, and only 9 of the 26 markets currently designated emerging by the IFC (Argentina, Brazil, Chile, Greece, Mexico, India, South Korea, Thailand, and Zimbabwe) have performance data for the entire time. In fact, historical results for another 7 of the emerging markets (China, Hungary, Indonesia, Peru, Poland, South Africa, and Sri Lanka) are available for fewer than 10 years (starting dates for inclusion in the EMDB are given in the first column of Table 1). Even though the limited historical data for emerging markets do not offer the investor the luxury of drawing conclusions from long-term empirically validated relationships, the data do offer investors important information about how emerging markets react to events, interact among themselves, and relate to developed markets.

Aggregate Returns and Risks

Table 4 presents comparative average monthly rates of return, computed both geometrically and arithmetically, and standard deviations of monthly returns for our Emerging Markets Composite Value-Weighted Index (the Composite), the S&P 500 Index, the National Association of Securities Dealers Automated Quotation Composite Index (Nasdaq), 91-day U.S. Treasury bills, and U.S. inflation in the form of the U.S. Consumer Price Index (CPI). Monthly emerging market returns are in the appendix.

Panel A of Table 4 presents results for the entire 1975–95 period. For the 20-year period, the performance of stocks in emerging markets trailed the returns for U.S. stocks.[1] The Composite provided a 0.99 percent compound average monthly rate of return, compared with the 1.11 percent return for the S&P 500 and the 1.07 percent return for the Nasdaq. Stocks in emerging markets fared well in comparison with T-bills and U.S. inflation. The 0.62 percent compound average monthly rate of return for T-bills was approximately two-thirds of the comparable return for emerging market stocks. Furthermore, the inflation rate for this period was less than one-half the average rate of return for emerging market stocks.

---

[1] The full period is 19½ years and the first subperiod is 9½ years, but when discussing results, for simplicity, we will refer to the periods in round numbers—as 20-, 10-, and 5-year periods.

Table 4. Series Historical Monthly Returns and Standard Deviations

A: December 1975–June 1995

Series	Arithmetic Average Return	Standard Deviation	Compound Average Return	Sharpe Index Values
Composite	1.15%	5.61%	0.99%	0.0945%
S&P 500	1.20	4.25	1.11	13.65
Nasdaq	1.21	5.26	1.07	11.22
T-bills	0.62	0.25	0.62	—
CPI	0.44	0.33	0.44	—

B: June 1985–June 1995

Series	Arithmetic Average Return	Standard Deviation	Compound Average Return	Sharpe Index Values
Composite	1.73%	6.65%	1.50%	18.80%
S&P 500	1.23	4.38	1.13	17.12
Nasdaq	1.11	5.31	0.96	11.86
T-bills	0.48	0.15	0.48	—
CPI	0.30	0.23	0.30	—

C: June 1990–June 1995

Series	Arithmetic Average Return	Standard Deviation	Compound Average Return	Sharpe Index Values
Composite	1.00%	5.66%	0.84%	10.78%
S&P 500	0.99	3.30	0.93	18.18
Nasdaq	1.30	4.89	1.18	18.61
T-bills	0.39	0.13	0.39	—
CPI	0.29	0.22	0.29	—

Figure 1 graphically portrays the growth for the 20-year period of a dollar invested in each asset class and a hypothetical asset returning the U.S. inflation rate. Table 5 summarizes the results for the 20-year period: US$1.00 invested in the Composite grew to US$10.01 at June 30, 1995, but the same amount invested in the S&P 500 grew to US$13.14 and in the Nasdaq grew to US$12.03.

As would be expected, emerging market stocks experienced greater variability of returns in the full period than did U.S. equities, as the last column in Panel A of Table 4 shows. The 5.61 percent monthly standard deviation of returns for the Composite exceeded the monthly standard deviation for the S&P 500 (4.25 percent) and for the Nasdaq (5.26 percent) for the period, although the margin may be lower than many investors would have expected.

The return and risk results reported here for 1975 through 1995 contradict conventional wisdom that higher risk emerging market stocks provide higher rates of return than stocks in developed markets. For example, Claessens, Dasgupta, and Glen (1995) reported higher average returns for the IFC's Composite Index of emerging market securities than for the United States, Japan, and the Morgan Stanley Capital International World Index. One reason for the different results is that most of the recent studies of emerging market performance have focused on the post-1984 period because 1984 was the base year for the IFC's value-weighted indexes. We believe, however, that limiting data to the period following the debt crisis in Latin America severely biases results by omitting a period in which one of the risks of investing in the markets was indeed realized.

The results here present an obvious problem to investors. If the stocks of emerging markets provide lower rates of return at higher risk than domestic securities, they are not particularly attractive additions to broadly diversified portfolios.

Figure 1 shows, however, that emerging markets experienced vastly different results during the first 10 years as opposed to the remaining 10 years of the period.

Figure 1. **Performance of Composite versus Various Asset Classes and the CPI, December 1975–June 1995**

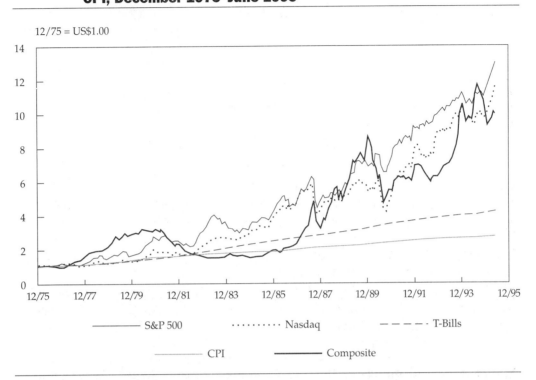

Structural changes have occurred in the markets since 1984, and again since 1989, and the Composite during the initial years consisted of a narrower, less diversified set of securities than later. Consequently, in addition to the full period, we also analyzed the most recent 10-year and 5-year periods.

The 1985–95 Subperiod. Performance results dramatically reversed during the 10-year period from June 1985 through June 1995. In contrast to the 1975–95 performance results, in the 1985–95 period, emerging market stocks exhibited higher rates of return than their U.S. counterparts. As shown in Panel B of Table 4, for the later 10-year period, the Composite returned 1.50 percent compounded monthly, compared with 1.13 percent for the S&P 500 and 0.96 percent for the Nasdaq. Figure 2 shows the wealth increase of a dollar invested as previously, and Table 5 summarizes the results: During this decade, a wealth index of the Composite appreciated sixfold, thus substantially outperforming the S&P 500's increase of 3.79 times and the Nasdaq's advance of 2.92 times. (A dollar invested in emerging stocks in mid-1985 grew to US$6.00 by June 1995, compared with growth to US$3.87 for the S&P 500 and US$3.15 for the Nasdaq.

As Panel B of Table 4 shows, the higher rates of return in emerging markets in the 1985–95 period were accompanied by higher variability of returns. The 6.65 percent monthly standard deviation of returns for the Composite exceeded the 4.38 percent monthly standard deviation for the S&P 500 and the 5.31 percent monthly standard deviation for the Nasdaq. The standard deviation in this decade was also higher than in the full period, in spite of the fact that a larger number of markets and companies were included in the database in these later years.

The 1990–95 Period. During the most recent five-year period, as Panel C in

Table 5.   Index Values as of End of June 1995

Market	US$1.00 Invested at Year-End 1975[a]	US$1.00 Invested at end of June 1985[b]
Composite	US$10.01[c]	US$6.00[c]
S&P 500	13.14	3.87
Nasdaq	12.03	3.15
T-bills	4.24	1.78
CPI	2.78	1.43

[a]Data had to start before July 1985 to be included in this column.

[b]Data had to start before July 1990 to be included in this column.

[c]Values of the Composite in an average of local currencies were 107.25 for one unit of local currency invested at year-end 1975 and 19.42 for one unit of local currency invested at mid-year 1985.

Table 4 indicates, stocks in emerging markets experienced lower rates of return than U.S. stocks. From June 1990 through June 1995, the Composite recorded a 0.84 percent compound monthly rate of return, compared with a return of 0.93 percent for the S&P 500 and 1.18 percent for the Nasdaq. As shown in Figure 3, during this period, US$1.00 invested in the Composite grew to US$1.66, compared with US$1.75 for the S&P 500 and US$2.02 for the Nasdaq.

Table 4 also shows that volatility was higher for the emerging market stocks than for U.S. stocks in this period. The monthly standard deviation of the Composite for June 1990 through June 1995 was 5.66 percent, compared with 4.89 percent for the Nasdaq and 3.30 percent for the S&P 500.

Figure 2.   Performance of Composite versus Various Asset Classes and the CPI, June 1985–June 1995

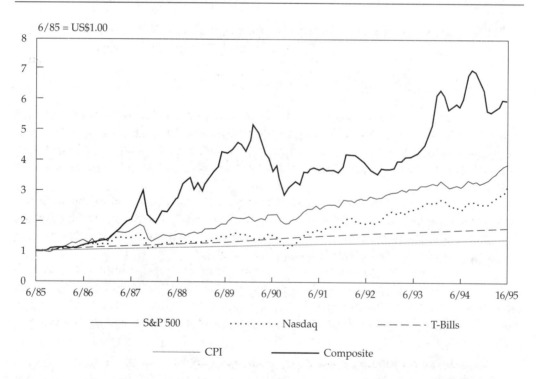

©The Research Foundation of the ICFA

Figure 3.   Performance of Composite versus Various Asset Classes and the CPI, June 1990–June 1995

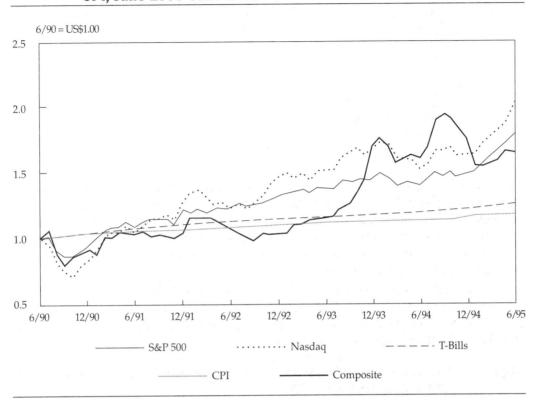

Risk-Adjusted Returns. To calculate risk-adjusted rates of return for securities in the aggregate series, we used Sharpe's Portfolio Performance Index:

$$\text{Sharpe Index} = \frac{\text{Asset's average rate of return} - \text{Riskless rate of return}}{\text{Asset's standard deviation of returns}}.$$

The results reveal that for the 1985–95 period, emerging market stocks provided higher rates of return than U.S. stocks after adjustment for risk. Calculated using monthly data, the Sharpe Index for emerging markets stocks equaled 18.80 percent, which exceeded the Sharpe Index for the S&P 500 (17.12 percent) and the Nasdaq (11.86 percent).

Stocks in emerging markets underperformed U.S. stocks on a risk-adjusted basis, however, in the period from June 1990 through June 1995. The Sharpe Index for the Composite was 10.78 percent, only approximately one-half the Sharpe Index for the S&P 500 (18.18 percent) or the Nasdaq (18.61 percent).

Table 4 shows that during the entire time period from December 1975 through June 1995, emerging markets underperformed U.S. stocks on a risk-adjusted basis. The Sharpe Index for the composite was 9.45 percent, about two-thirds the Sharpe Index for the S&P 500 (13.65 percent) and closer to the Nasdaq Sharpe Index value of 11.22 percent.

Summary of Findings from Aggregate Series. The poor relative performance of emerging market stocks from the end of 1975 through 1995 seems to contradict the popular belief among many investors that emerging market securities are an attractive asset class with high expected rates of return and strong diversification benefits. Although the diversification benefit was indeed available during this period, the emerging market stocks underperformed U.S. stocks.

The underperformance of emerging market assets in the overall time period is largely attributable to poor relative performance during the five years ending in 1985—a time period during which the emerging markets were substantially smaller and less developed than they currently are. A large part of that performance must be associated with the global recession of late 1980 through 1982, when interest rates hit record highs and oil prices soared. Those events precipitated the Latin American debt crisis, and they are reflected in the results reported here. The four years beginning in December 1980 could be called the "lost years" of the emerging equity markets.

From 1985 to 1995, stocks in emerging markets fared favorably relative to U.S. stock markets on an absolute and on a risk-adjusted basis. The relative overperformance of the emerging market stocks in later subperiods would have been even more pronounced if the crash in certain Latin American markets had not occurred in late 1994 and early 1995.

The dramatic reversal of the fortunes of emerging market stocks during the most recent decade creates a dilemma for investors. Does this performance prove that investments in emerging markets truly provide the often-touted benefits of high expected rates of return and overall portfolio risk reduction through enhanced diversification? Or will investments in this evolving asset class continue to experience the kind of dramatic reversals of fortune observed during the past 20 years? Only time will tell. Even during this recent period of relative prosperity among emerging market equities, erratic price swings were frequent. No fewer than three major bear markets occurred for these securities during the recent decade (late 1987, 1989, and 1994–95) versus only one major decline in U.S. stocks (October 1987). Given the relatively short span of time in which data regarding the performance of these assets have been available, however, it is probably too early to use empirical performance results to conclusively support either side of this question. One conclusion seems certain: Equities in emerging markets will continue to experience substantial price fluctuations. Thus, considering these securities as strictly long-term holdings is imperative.

In the remainder of this chapter, we consider the importance of currency issues and then take currency issues into account as we present detailed empirical results and analyses of the performance of emerging market stocks by region and by individual country market.

The Currency Factor

Investing in an emerging market exposes the investor to the market's currency values. The currency, in turn, is exposed to political risk and a host of economic influences. Indeed, at least a portion of the interest the developed world has shown in the securities of emerging markets has come as a result of fundamental changes in monetary and fiscal policies on the part of emerging market governments that affect currency values. For example, investor interest in Argentina increased dramatically in March 1991 after the Carlos Menem administration adopted a currency board and a "convertibility" plan under which the government stood ready to buy and sell U.S. dollars at a rate of one Argentine peso to the dollar. Pesos would be printed only to the extent that they were fully backed by U.S. dollar reserves. During that same year, as noted in the Introduction, the Argentine stock market achieved the highest rate of return in the world, a return in excess of 400 percent. To achieve the currency stability, the country had to adopt a new economic platform to eliminate government budget deficits and stabilize the economy. Brazil followed Argentina's lead in July 1994, and global investor interest in the Brazilian markets rapidly increased.

The currency risk factor is well known. Anyone prone to forget about it was rudely reminded in December 1994 when the Mexican peso collapsed, losing more than half of its value. Mexico was thrown into a broad economic crisis in which inflation returned to past high levels, interest rates soared, and economic growth was reversed. Indexes of equity values for stocks traded on the Bolsa Mexicana de Valores fell more than 50 percent in the ensuing weeks, and the markets of some of the other Latin American economies (notably, Argentina and Brazil) also declined sharply.[2]

Currency issues are also relevant from another point of view. Equity market performance may look quite different to a domestic investor than it looks to a global investor. A global investor's opportunities to diversify away the risk of a given market's currency may give that investor quite a different outlook from the outlook of a domestic investor, particularly if the domestic investor is restricted from investing in foreign securities. On the other hand, some emerging markets are removing or decreasing restrictions against investing in foreign securities, so domestic investors in those markets now need to know the performance of a broader set of prospective investments than concerned them in the past. For example, Chile's privately managed pension funds were granted the right to invest in foreign equities in 1994, and although as of late 1995 no specific vehicles for such investment had been approved, as Chileans consider investment outside Chile, they will need to broaden their views of performance appraisal.

Because the currency risk factor is crucial to the decision to invest in emerging markets, performance of the 26 emerging markets in the study is presented here in both local currency terms and in U.S. dollar terms. The goals are to demonstrate for the reader the impact of the currency factor on performance and to give domestic investors in the emerging markets a sense of how their markets stack up against other markets.

The Fallacy of Cross-Currency Comparisons of Portfolios. Comparing performance in alternative currencies rather than in a single currency can produce misleading results. For example, Panel A of Figure 4 shows that Chile's performance since 1975 in Chilean peso terms so dominated South Korea's performance in won terms that the Korean index is indistinguishable from the horizontal axis. Panel B shows, however, that when a common currency is used—in this case, the U.S. dollar—although Chile still dominated in total returns, the margin, still huge by the end of the period, was not so wide. Figure 5 examines a case in which performance is reversed: Mexico versus India. In the local currency numbers used in Panel A, Mexico dominated India so much that India (like Korea in the previous example) is virtually flat by comparison. In the U.S. dollar terms of Panel B, however, the performances of the two markets are virtually identical at the end of the period (mid-1995). Panel B in Figure 5 also illustrates that relative performance is highly sensitive to the time period selected: If the analysis were stopped shortly before the Mexican peso crisis, Mexico's performance would be substantially stronger than that of Korea. The shock effect of the peso crisis wiped out all of Mexico's comparative gain prior to the crisis.

---

[2]Bailey and Chung (1995) evaluated the currency risk and political risk associated with Mexican debt and equity securities. Unfortunately, their study's data concluded in 1994 before the crisis in the peso in December of that year. Nevertheless, their results demonstrate the importance of currency and political risk factors in the pricing of securities.

Figure 4. Performance of Chile versus Korea: Local Currency and U.S. Dollar Terms, December 1975–June 1994

A: Local Currency Terms

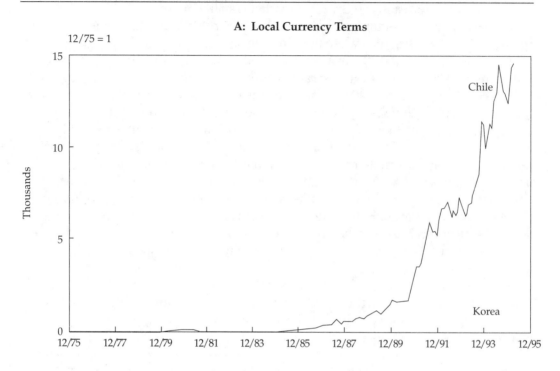

B: U.S. Dollar Terms

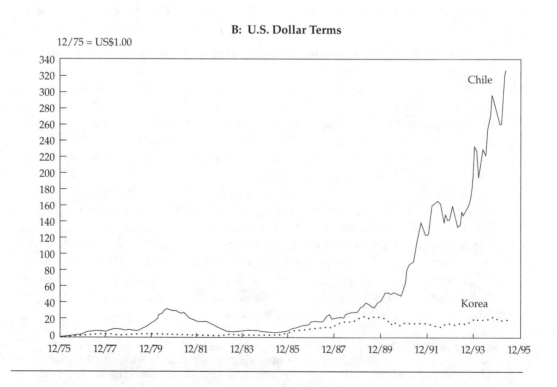

Figure 5. Performance of India versus Mexico: Local Currency and U.S. Dollar Terms, December 1975–June 1995

A: Local Currency Terms

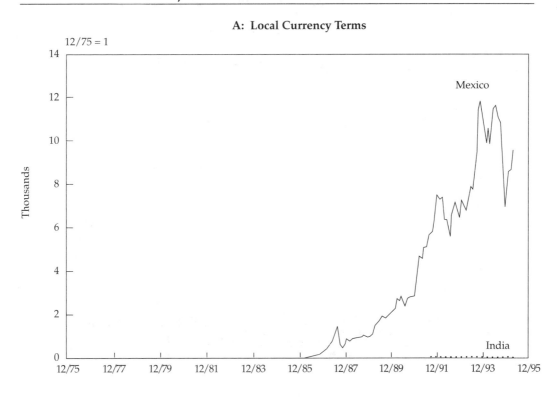

B: U.S. Dollar Terms

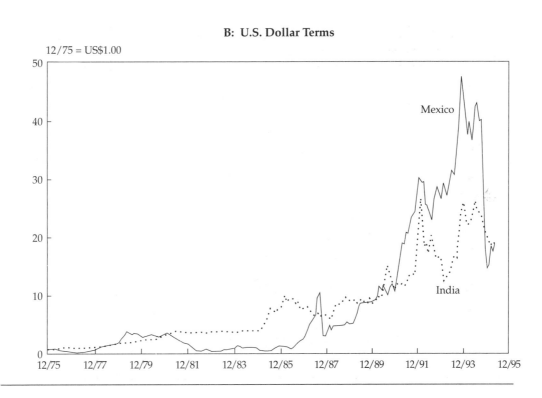

Thus, currency values are very important to the performance of alternative markets. In the next section, we display currency values across all of the markets in our sample for varying time periods. While reading this section, readers should keep the time sensitivity in mind.

Performance by Geographical Region and Market

To provide greater detail about the performance of emerging markets by various geographical regions, we constructed a series of subindexes—for Europe, Latin America, Asia (and also separately for East Asia and South Asia), Africa, and a combined Europe/Mideast/Africa (EMA) area. The findings are reported in local currency and U.S. dollar terms.

Tables 6, 7, and 8 show local currency versus U.S. dollar arithmetic average monthly returns, standard deviations of monthly returns, and compound returns for, respectively, the 20-year, 10-year, and 5-year periods. Table 9 shows the wealth accumulation of US$1.00 or one unit of local currency invested in the regional and country markets between December 1975 and June 1995; Table 10 reports similarly for investments made between June 1985 and June 1995. The regions and country markets included in the tables are those for which performance data for the period were available. For some markets, data were not available for some of the periods; if

Table 6.   Monthly Mean Returns, Standard Deviations, and Compound Average Returns in U.S. Dollar Terms versus Local Currency Terms: Markets with Data Available December 1975–June 1995

	U.S. Dollar Terms			Local Currency Terms		
Market	Arithmetic Average Return	Standard Deviation	Compound Average Return	Arithmetic Average Return	Standard Deviation	Compound Average Return
Composite	1.15%	5.61%	0.99%	2.17%	5.56%	2.02%
EMA	0.75	7.15	0.50	1.74	6.78	1.52
Europe	0.78	9.32	0.37	1.96	8.81	1.60
Greece	0.68	9.97	0.23	1.43	9.56	1.03
Jordan	1.05	5.26	0.91	1.42	5.13	1.30
Africa	0.44	9.95	−0.07	1.87	7.52	1.58
Nigeria	1.41	15.85	0.03	3.86	4.27	3.78
Zimbabwe	1.17	10.02	0.68	2.27	9.74	1.81
Latin America	1.95	9.01	1.53	5.32	9.00	4.93
Argentina	5.61	30.25	2.11	15.55	41.20	10.45
Brazil	2.31	18.49	0.70	15.37	28.47	12.70
Chile	3.08	11.03	2.51	4.71	10.78	4.18
Colombia	3.31	9.03	2.95	5.12	9.13	4.75
Mexico	2.20	12.91	1.27	4.69	11.92	4.00
Venezuela	1.75	13.14	0.88	4.03	11.60	3.40
Asia	1.38	6.14	1.20	1.55	6.05	1.37
East Asia	1.86	9.54	1.43	1.98	9.40	1.56
Korea	1.69	9.00	1.32	1.88	8.89	1.51
Philippines	3.68	10.65	3.14	3.91	11.07	3.35
Taiwan	2.83	14.77	1.79	2.46	14.48	1.45
South Asia	1.30	5.29	1.16	1.56	5.24	1.43
India	1.55	7.87	1.26	2.11	8.17	1.80
Malaysia	1.46	7.82	1.15	1.47	7.88	1.15
Pakistan	1.60	6.96	1.38	2.17	7.02	1.95
Thailand	1.95	7.82	1.65	2.03	7.77	1.73

Note: Data had to start before July 1985 to be included in this table.

Table 7. Monthly Mean Returns, Standard Deviations, and Compound Average Returns in U.S. Dollar Terms versus Local Currency Terms: Markets with Data Available June 1985–June 1995

	U.S. Dollar Terms			Local Currency Terms		
Market	Arithmetic Average Return	Standard Deviation	Compound Average Return	Arithmetic Average Return	Standard Deviation	Compound Average Return
Composite	1.73%	6.65%	1.50%	2.73%	6.78%	2.50%
EMA	1.55	8.97	1.17	2.85	8.58	2.50
Europe	2.50	11.50	1.88	3.74	11.03	3.18
Greece	2.32	12.55	1.61	2.71	12.33	2.04
Portugal	2.63	12.77	1.92	2.57	12.63	1.87
Turkey	4.03	21.15	2.05	7.99	20.57	0.09
Jordan	0.63	4.88	0.51	1.09	4.84	0.98
Africa	1.16	9.86	0.63	3.16	4.21	3.07
Nigeria	1.47	16.24	0.02	3.96	4.34	3.88
Zimbabwe	1.69	8.58	1.33	3.09	8.11	2.77
Latin America	3.11	9.12	2.68	7.53	9.46	7.10
Argentina	5.76	28.91	2.70	16.37	46.65	10.89
Brazil	3.43	22.64	1.02	23.25	35.67	19.21
Chile	3.82	8.07	3.51	4.55	7.73	4.26
Colombia	3.54	9.19	3.16	5.25	9.33	4.86
Mexico	3.46	13.83	2.38	6.16	13.59	5.24
Venezuela	1.70	13.46	0.79	4.10	11.88	3.44
Asia	1.58	7.32	1.31	1.53	7.29	1.26
East Asia	2.40	9.63	1.94	2.15	9.43	1.71
Korea	2.03	8.55	1.68	1.89	8.42	1.56
Philippines	3.68	10.84	3.12	3.99	11.31	3.40
Taiwan	3.11	15.08	2.03	2.71	14.79	1.66
South Asia	1.36	6.15	1.17	1.59	6.28	1.39
India	1.27	9.64	0.82	2.10	10.33	1.60
Indonesia	0.44	8.89	0.05	0.68	8.86	0.30
Malaysia	1.54	7.96	1.22	1.52	8.02	1.20
Pakistan	1.59	7.11	1.36	2.16	7.18	1.92
Thailand	2.69	9.09	2.28	2.61	9.15	2.19

Note: Data had to start before July 1990 to be included in this table.

a market was included in the EMDB before the end of the given period, that market is included in the table with results based on that portion of the period for which data were available. (Beginning dates for a market's inclusion in the EMDB are given in Table 1.) Comparing the "U.S. Dollar" set of columns with the "Local Currency" set of columns reveals the performance in the different terms for each period. Table 11 shows the performance of the currencies themselves in U.S. dollar terms—that is, the compound average gain or loss in value in U.S. dollars of each market's currency (or an average of a region's currencies) over the three periods.

Note first the currency effect on emerging markets in the aggregate. Table 6 provides results for the full 20-year period. Note that for the Composite, monthly average performance was considerably higher when measured in local currency terms than when measured in U.S. dollar terms. Both the arithmetic returns and geometric returns were about 100 basis points a month lower in U.S. dollar terms. In effect, emerging market currencies lost about 1 percent of their value a month over the full 20-year period. Table 11 confirms that conclusion: The Composite emerging market "currency" lost 1.008 percent of its value a month, on average, over this period.

Table 8. Monthly Mean Returns, Standard Deviations, and Compound Average Returns in U.S. Dollar Terms versus Local Currency Terms: Markets with Data Available June 1990–June 1995

Market	U.S. Dollar Terms			Local Currency Terms		
	Arithmetic Average Return	Standard Deviation	Compound Average Return	Arithmetic Average Return	Standard Deviation	Compound Average Return
Composite	1.00%	5.66%	0.84%	2.44%	5.87%	2.27%
EMA	0.31	7.73	0.01	1.62	7.37	1.36
Europe	−0.21	9.03	−0.60	1.77	8.74	1.41
Greece	−0.62	8.63	−0.98	−0.06	9.02	−0.44
Hungary	1.02	14.67	0.18	2.38	15.00	1.50
Poland	8.13	25.70	5.51	10.08	27.19	7.19
Portugal	0.34	6.48	0.14	0.35	5.67	0.20
Turkey	0.52	17.88	−0.99	5.05	16.77	0.15
Jordan	0.92	4.60	0.81	0.99	4.50	0.89
Africa	1.52	10.65	0.97	2.89	5.10	2.77
Nigeria	2.81	19.95	0.71	4.84	4.37	4.76
South Africa	2.40	7.34	2.14	1.13	5.20	0.99
Zimbabwe	0.34	10.45	−0.20	2.39	10.20	1.88
Latin America	2.25	7.48	1.98	6.75	7.79	6.47
Argentina	3.51	17.58	2.31	4.81	19.33	3.38
Brazil	3.12	16.52	1.87	24.04	25.00	21.66
Chile	3.41	8.05	3.10	3.84	7.55	3.57
Colombia	3.83	11.35	3.26	5.14	11.69	4.54
Mexico	1.50	10.82	0.87	2.59	8.92	2.20
Peru	3.57	13.74	2.67	4.64	13.92	3.73
Venezuela	1.71	13.52	0.85	3.85	13.37	3.02
Asia	0.84	6.63	0.62	0.92	6.70	0.70
East Asia	0.59	8.31	0.25	0.60	8.21	0.27
China	0.47	23.99	−1.67	0.54	23.56	−1.52
Korea	0.64	7.87	0.35	0.76	7.81	0.47
Philippines	2.03	10.02	1.55	2.25	10.08	1.77
Taiwan	1.05	13.17	0.25	0.96	13.11	0.16
South Asia	1.37	6.48	1.17	1.58	6.70	1.37
India	1.59	10.96	1.03	2.70	12.12	2.03
Indonesia	−0.13	8.69	−0.50	0.10	8.66	−0.27
Malaysia	1.65	7.52	1.37	1.49	7.79	1.19
Pakistan	2.23	9.57	1.82	2.85	9.71	2.42
Sri Lanka	0.89	9.83	0.43	1.18	9.82	0.72
Thailand	1.83	9.85	1.37	1.77	9.99	1.30

In other words, approximately 50 percent of the performance (in local currency terms) of emerging markets over the full period was wiped out by declining currency values. The currency effect is indeed important in the analysis of emerging stock markets.

The effect described in the previous paragraph is relatively stable over time, at least at the aggregate (Composite) level: Comparing the returns in Tables 7 and 8 for the Composite index reveals that, again, a large fraction of the overall performance of emerging markets in local currency terms has been erased by the poor performance of their currencies against the U.S. dollar. In the case of the 10-year period, presented in Table 7, about 40 percent of the compound return of emerging markets was eliminated by declines in currency values. In the five-year period, shown in Table 8, somewhat more than 60 percent of local performance was eliminated by the currency effect vis-à-vis the U.S. dollar.

Table 9.   Country and Region Index Values as of July 1995 Based on All Data Available December 1975–June 1995

Market	US$1.00 Invested	1 Unit of Local Currency Invested
EMA	3.23	34.44
Europe	2.37	41.02
Greece	1.72	10.88
Jordan	6.68	14.79
Africa	0.84	39.49
Nigeria	1.04	107.33
Zimbabwe	4.84	66.31
Latin America	35.06	77,121.77
Argentina	133.06	12,614,237,215.55
Brazil	5.11	1,406,319,309,360.73
Chile	331.36	14,590.48
Colombia	38.90	347.43
Mexico	19.17	9,590.59
Venezuela	3.00	67.93
Asia	16.18	24.03
East Asia	27.70	37.01
Korea	21.30	33.33
Philippines	49.34	63.83
Taiwan	9.40	6.16
South Asia	14.80	27.60
India	18.54	65.09
Malaysia	4.21	4.23
Pakistan	5.62	11.33
Thailand	45.82	55.47

Note: Data had to start before July 1985 to be included in this table.

The results vary sharply by region of the globe, and the variations are relatively stable for the periods of time examined. For example, Table 6 reveals that Latin America exhibited the highest compound average returns of any region in local currency terms in the 1975–95 period—and by a wide margin. In U.S. dollar terms, however, Latin America registered a performance only slightly better than East Asia's. Similar results are shown in Table 7 for the 10-year period ending in 1995, except that the margin in both local currency and U.S. dollar terms is greater for Latin America in this case. Finally, very similar results can be seen for the five-year period ending in 1995. (The similarity of results is, of course, less surprising because the periods overlap. The final section of this chapter presents results for separate 10-year periods that demonstrate, among other things, that Latin America *underperformed* East Asia and South Asia in U.S. dollar terms in the initial 10 years of the study period.)

In summary, nearly all of the emerging markets' currencies declined in value, on average, through the three time periods. And some performed spectacularly badly. For example, Brazilian currencies lost a compound average of 10.6 percent of their value *a month* against the U.S. dollar during the full 20-year period. In essence, the U.S. dollar multiplied in value against a series of Brazilian currencies by a factor of 275 *billion* times over the full period of these data. Accordingly, Brazilian monetary authorities have replaced currencies by computing them to new bases (usually, dividing by 1,000) five times during the period.

Table 10. Country and Region Index Values as of July 1995 Based on All Data Available June 1985– June 1995

Market	US$1.00 Invested	1 Unit of Local Currency Invested
EMA	4.02	19.39
Europe	9.38	42.72
Greece	6.83	11.33
Portugal	8.57	8.08
Turkey	7.94	1.09
Jordan	1.85	3.22
Africa	2.13	37.80
Nigeria	1.03	95.80
Zimbabwe	4.86	26.54
Latin America	23.87	3,737.80
Argentina	24.39	242,998.93
Brazil	3.38	1,432,166,504.85
Chile	62.72	150.06
Colombia	41.83	297.80
Mexico	16.83	461.27
Venezuela	2.56	58.04
Asia	4.78	4.51
East Asia	10.02	7.67
Korea	7.36	6.38
Philippines	40.08	55.49
Taiwan	11.11	7.18
South Asia	4.03	5.24
India	2.68	6.75
Indonesia	1.03	1.22
Malaysia	4.27	4.18
Pakistan	5.06	9.81
Thailand	14.91	13.43

Note: Data had to start before July 1990 to be included in this table.

Argentina's case is very different. Until 1991, Argentina underwent frequent currency devaluations of magnitudes similar to Brazil's. Since 1991, however, the Argentine peso has maintained its value against the U.S. dollar at 1-to-1 and government policy has brought inflation down to the level found in developed nations. Not surprisingly, Brazil introduced a system of currency management similar to that of Argentina when it introduced the Brazilian real in July 1994.

Both the Brazilian real and the Argentine peso withstood enormous pressure after the Mexican peso crisis of December 1994. The Brazilian real declined in value but stabilized; the Argentine peso was maintained at its constant exchange rate. The Mexican peso crisis was a tough test for these two relatively new currencies, but both passed the test.

Mexico's devaluations of 1976, 1982, and 1994 are well known to most U.S. investors. Investors may be surprised, therefore, that the Mexican peso has performed marginally better than the average emerging market currency in the period from July 1990 through June 1995. The peso was managed on a "crawling-peg" basis throughout the regime of Carlos Salinas (Mexican president from 1988 to 1994). Hence, the devaluation of 1994 was highly visible, but for the broader period, the peso performed about as well as other emerging market currencies.

Table 11 shows that only the currency of Taiwan increased in value against the

Table 11. Performance of Emerging Market Currencies in Terms of U.S. Dollars

Market	All Data since December 1975[a]	All Data since June 1985[b]	All Data since June 1990
Composite	−1.008%	−0.974%	−1.396%
EMA	−1.006	−1.302	−1.330
Europe	−1.212	−1.256	−1.982
Greece	−0.784	−0.421	−0.541
Hungary	—	—	−1.299
Poland	—	—	−1.566
Portugal	—	0.052	−0.059
Turkey	—	1.965	−1.136
Jordan	−0.379	−0.463	−0.078
Africa	−1.632	−2.366	−1.746
Nigeria	−3.613	−3.709	−3.857
South Africa	—	—	1.136
Zimbabwe	−1.112	−1.405	−2.045
Latin America	−3.235	−4.124	−4.216
Argentina	−7.549	−7.385	−1.038
Brazil	−10.646	−15.257	−16.265
Chile	−1.604	−0.724	−0.451
Colombia	−1.723	−1.622	−1.228
Mexico	−2.621	−2.722	−1.301
Peru	—	—	−1.025
Venezuela	−2.446	−2.566	−2.114
Asia	−0.169	0.049	−0.080
East Asia	−0.124	0.224	−0.018
China	—	—	−0.159
Korea	−0.191	0.119	−0.116
Philippines	−0.204	−0.271	−0.215
Taiwan	0.336	0.364	0.086
South Asia	−0.266	−0.220	−0.199
India	−0.535	−0.769	−0.982
Indonesia	—	−0.246	−0.227
Malaysia	−0.004	0.018	0.176
Pakistan	−0.555	−0.549	−0.592
Sri Lanka	—	—	−0.292
Thailand	−0.082	0.087	0.068

[a]Data had to start before July 1985 to be included in this column.
[b]Data had to start before July 1990 to be included in this column.

dollar on a sustained basis in the three time periods. Malaysia and Thailand experienced gains in their currencies' values against the dollar over the 10-year period ending in June 1995. Most other markets experienced serious depreciation in the values of their currencies against the U.S. dollar. The cases of South Africa, Taiwan, Malaysia, and Thailand illustrate, however, that "emerging" is not synonymous with "currency falling in value."

In addition to analyzing the effects of currency on relative returns for evaluation purposes, investors should be wary of interpreting results based on any single currency, even the U.S. dollar. In the decade after mid-1985, a period during which the United States experienced large fiscal and trade deficits, the dollar itself declined in value against the currencies of other major developed markets. From the end of June 1985 through the end of June 1996, the dollar fell nearly 50 percent against the

French franc, more than 50 percent against both the German mark and Japanese yen, and 30 percent against the British pound. A 50 percent decline over 11 years translates into a compound average decline of about 0.52 percent a month. Declining currency values are not unique to emerging markets.

The poor performance of the U.S. dollar in the 1985–96 period provokes a warning to readers outside the United States: Performance results in this monograph are presented only in U.S. dollar terms or local currency terms. Therefore, the returns overstate the performance of emerging markets against currencies in some other developed nations, notably, Japan, Germany, France, and the United Kingdom.[3]

The following sections summarize the performance of emerging markets in terms of wealth accumulation in the various regional and country markets. As previously, if a market was included in the EMDB before the end of the five-year period relevant to the table, that market is included in the table with results based on the portion of the period for which data were available. (Beginning dates for a market's inclusion in the EMDB are given in Table 1.)

Europe. Figure 6 reveals that the stocks of the European emerging markets (Greece, Hungary, Poland, Portugal, and Turkey) have been unable to keep up with U.S. inflation, largely because of extremely weak performance results from 1980 through 1985. For the entire period from 1975 through June 1995, US$1.00 invested in an index of the stocks of European emerging markets would have advanced only to US$2.37, less than one-third the value for the S&P 500 (US$13.14 from Table 5).

■ *Greece.* Greek stocks, which have been included in the EMDB since its inception, have performed poorly. As reported in Table 9, US$1.00 invested in Greek stocks on December 31, 1975, had appreciated to only US$1.72 at June 30, 1995. Consequently, Greek equities not only substantially underperformed U.S. stocks (from Table 5, S&P 500 appreciation to US$13.14 and Nasdaq appreciation to US$12.03) but also failed to provide rates of return sufficient to offset U.S. inflation (from Table 5, CPI appreciation to US$2.78). In only one time period, five years ending June 1990, did Greek stocks provide unusually attractive rates of returns.

■ *Hungary.* Included in the EMDB only since December 31, 1992, Hungarian stocks have exhibited highly sporadic returns. A wealth index in Hungarian equities appreciated only 5 percent in U.S. dollar terms from year-end 1992 to midyear 1995, thus considerably underperforming the U.S. stock indexes and failing to keep up with U.S. inflation.

■ *Poland.* Polish equities recorded exceptionally strong results from the time of their inclusion in the EMDB on December 31, 1992, to early 1994. During this period, a wealth index of Polish stocks grew by a factor of almost 13. Subsequently, however, Polish stocks lost almost two-thirds of their total market values. Nevertheless, at June 30, 1995, this market still showed cumulative returns meaningfully in excess of the cumulative returns of U.S. equities.

■ *Portugal.* After approximately their first 1¾ years of inclusion in the EMDB, Portuguese stocks had appreciated approximately 20-fold. During the next 1½ years, however, Portuguese stocks relinquished more than two-thirds of these accumulated gains. Nevertheless, Table 10 indicates that by June 30, 1995, a US$1.00 investment made in July 1985 in Portuguese stocks had grown to US$8.57, more than double the

[3] Portfolio management and risk management techniques allow the investor to manage currency risk separately while incorporating a market play into the investor's portfolio. See, for example, Karnosky and Singer (1994).

Figure 6. Performance of European Emerging Markets versus Various Asset Classes and the CPI, December 1975–June 1995

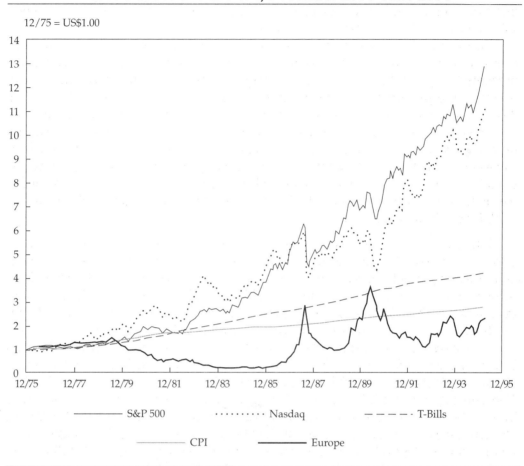

12/75 = US$1.00

value growth of a wealth index of the S&P 500 for the same period (US$3.87).

▨ *Turkey.* From the time of its inclusion in the EMDB at the end of 1986, the Turkish stock market exploded upward until mid-1990. Largely as a result of the Iraqi invasion of Kuwait, Turkish stock prices then collapsed during the following 1½ years. After strong price recoveries in 1993 and 1995, the wealth index of Turkish stocks resided at a level substantially above that of U.S. equities. From year-end 1986 through midyear 1995, US$1.00 invested in Turkish stocks grew to US$7.94 (see Table 10), as compared with US$3.87 for investing in the S&P 500.

Jordan. After experiencing healthy rates of return from 1979 to 1981, Jordanian stocks struggled through a decade of virtually no value growth. Only since 1992 have Jordanian equities resumed their upward price movement, interrupted only by a 1994 price setback. Primarily as a result of the stagnant market from 1982 through 1991, the wealth index of Jordan stocks did not keep pace with U.S. equities. The wealth index for Jordan by midyear 1995 (US$6.68 for the full period, see Table 9) was approximately 50 percent below the wealth index of the S&P 500 index (US$13.14).

Latin America. The Latin American subindex consists of seven emerging markets: Argentina, Brazil, Chile, Colombia, Mexico, Peru, and Venezuela. As portrayed in Figure 7, rates of return for Latin American equities showed considerable

Figure 7. Performance of Latin American Emerging Markets versus Various Asset Classes and the CPI, December 1975–June 1995

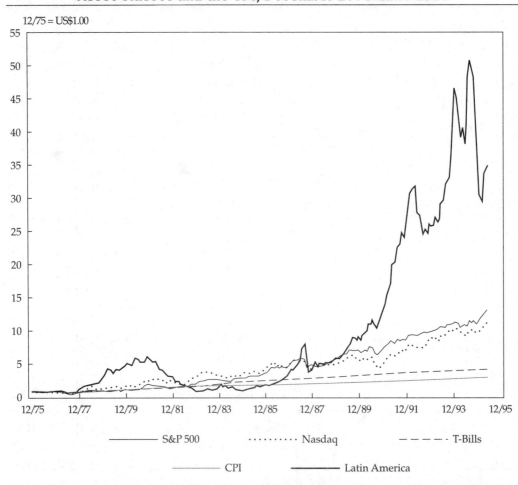

variability while, from 1976 through 1985, substantially underperforming the U.S. stock markets, U.S. T-bills, and U.S. inflation. In the most recent decade, however, Latin American equities experienced explosive returns. During this period, as Table 10 shows, a wealth index of Latin American stocks appreciated to US$23.87 in U.S. dollar terms, more than six times the rate of U.S. stocks as measured by the S&P 500 (US$3.87) and more than seven times the Nasdaq (US$3.15). The relative price performance of Latin American equities would have been even more spectacular without the "crash" during late 1994 and early 1995, which was largely concentrated among Mexican securities.

Wide variances in rates of return occurred among the individual Latin American markets. Chile and Argentina provided the highest rates of return among all the individual emerging markets; Brazil and Venezuela yielded among the worst returns of all the markets. Some of the most violent price swings in the emerging markets occurred among Latin American securities.

■ *Argentina.* Argentine equities experienced highly variable returns for 1976 through June 1995, as Table 6 shows. By the early part of 1980, the index of Argentine stocks had soared almost 50-fold—a remarkable performance, especially when considering that U.S. stock returns were lethargic during this time period. By the end of 1984, however, Argentine stocks had relinquished virtually all of this appreciation.

From that point on, Argentine stocks began a dramatic, but erratic, price surge. By June 1995 (see Table 9), the Argentine stock index stood at 133 times its December 1975 value, having at one point during 1992 peaked at over 200 times its initial value. Argentina's stock market provided the second highest returns among all emerging markets, even during a time of rampant inflation throughout the Argentine economy. Table 9 shows that in local currency terms, by June 30, 1995, Argentine stocks had appreciated more that 12.6 billion times their year-end 1975 value.

■ *Brazil*. In local currency terms, a wealth index composed of Brazilian stocks appreciated an astounding 1.4 trillion times from December 31, 1975, to June 30, 1995 (see Table 9). This enormous appreciation did not translate, however, to attractive rates of return for foreign investors. Measured in U.S. dollars, Brazilian stocks showed only a 5.11 times appreciation over this period. The wealth index of Brazilian stocks was at only approximately 60 percent of the level of the S&P 500's wealth index at June 30, 1995 (at US$13.14) and only slightly surpassed the wealth index of U.S. T-bills (at US$4.24). Note that stocks of Brazil's neighbor Argentina appreciated in value by more than 25 times the value of Brazilian stocks in U.S. dollar terms.

■ *Chile*. Largely as a result of its widely acclaimed transformation to a free-market economy, Chile recorded the highest stock market total returns among all emerging markets in the studied time period. Table 9 reports that US$1.00 invested in Chilean stocks at year-end 1975 appreciated to US$331.36 by mid-1995. Thus, a portfolio of Chilean stocks provided more than 20 times the value increase of a portfolio of U.S. equities (US$13.14 for the S&P 500 and US$12.03 for the Nasdaq). A large portion of the value growth in Chilean stocks occurred during the most recent decade, as Table 10 shows.

Chile provides an excellent example of the volatility of emerging market equities. Even within this remarkable stock growth spiral, erratic price swings occurred. For example, from mid-1980 to year-end 1984, Chilean stocks lost more than 90 percent of their market value. Stock prices soared thereafter, but even the rapid price appreciation during the recent decade was not without interruption; Chilean stocks experienced meaningful price declines during 1992, 1993, and 1994.

■ *Colombia*. Reported results of Colombian stock performance date back only to 1985. During the decade ended June 30, 1995, Colombian stocks significantly outperformed U.S. securities. As indicated in Table 10, a US$1.00 investment in Colombian stocks would have grown to US$41.83, more than 10-fold the growth of an investment in the S&P 500 (US$3.85) and more than 13 times the Nasdaq (US$3.15). Furthermore, of the emerging markets, only Chile recorded higher equity returns than Colombia during this period. Most of Colombia's stock market appreciation occurred during two time periods, late 1991 and early 1993 to early 1994. Like some other Latin American markets, Colombia suffered severe stock price declines during late 1994 and early 1995.

■ *Mexico*. In terms of market capitalization, Mexico is the largest market in Latin America. In terms of performance, Mexico has been among the most erratic. By year-end 1993, the Mexican stock market, riding on the North American Free Trade Agreement, had appreciated by almost 50 times its year-end 1975 value. However, as reported in Table 9, by mid-1995, the Mexican stock market was at only 19.17 times its year-end 1975 value. The devastating collapse of the Mexican market during 1994 and 1995 overshadowed the stock returns experienced previously. As Table 10 shows, even after accounting for the market collapse, Mexican stocks (at a growth of US$1.00 to US$16.83) outperformed their U.S. counterparts by more than fourfold (S&P 500 at US$3.87 and Nasdaq at US$3.15) during the decade ended June 30, 1995.

■ *Peru.* Peruvian stock performance data have been reported only since December 1992. During the brief period to 1995, Peruvian stocks performed well in comparison with U.S. securities. The stock market in Peru achieved a 2.67 percent monthly compound average rate of return while the U.S. market experienced a 0.93 percent compound average rate of return.

■ *Venezuela.* The stock market in Venezuela has not performed well relative to the U.S. markets. As indicated in Table 9, US$1.00 invested in Venezuelan stocks at December 31, 1984, would have grown to only US$3.00 by June 30, 1995. In contrast, the same investment in the S&P 500 would have appreciated to US$4.55. Venezuelan stock rates of return were the worst among all Latin American countries during the decade ended June 30, 1995; Table 8 indicates that the compound average monthly rate of return in U.S. dollars was only 0.85 percent as compared with 1.98 percent per month for the Latin America regional index.

Asia. The performance of the Asian emerging markets from 1975 to 1995 is depicted in Figure 8. For purposes of performance review, these markets are divided here into East Asia and South Asia subregions.

■ *East Asia.* The East Asian emerging markets consist of China, Korea, the Philippines, and Taiwan. Figure 9 graphically portrays the performance results for East

Figure 8. Performance of Asian Emerging Markets versus Various Asset Classes and the CPI, December 1975–June 1995

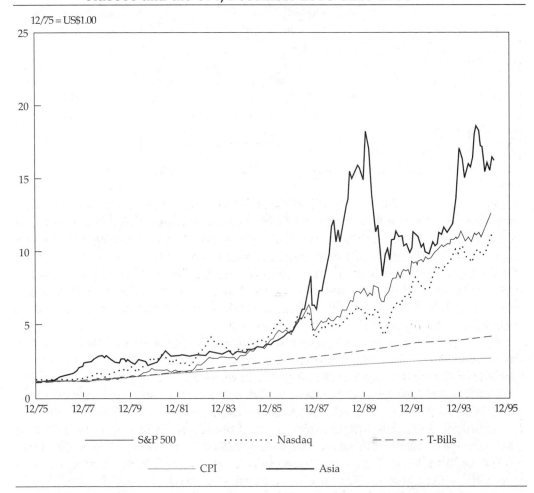

©The Research Foundation of the ICFA

Figure 9. Performance of East Asian Emerging Markets versus Various Asset Classes and the CPI, December 1975–June 1995

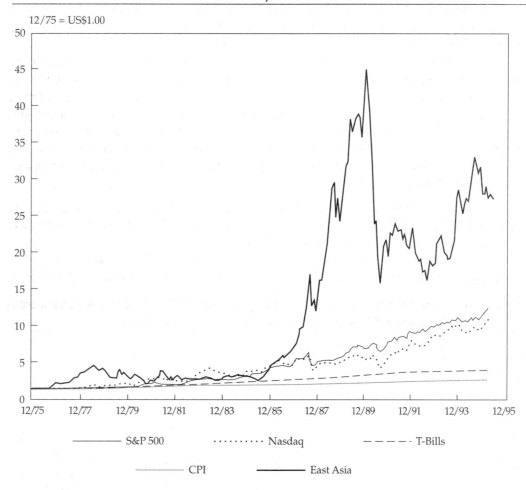

Asian stocks as compared with U.S. stocks, T-bills, and inflation. After experiencing modest returns from 1975 to 1984, East Asian stocks soared. From 1985 to 1989, a wealth index of these stocks increased in value by a factor of more than 20, only to lose approximately two-thirds of the accumulated value during the following nine months. After experiencing considerable price variability during the next five years, the wealth index of East Asian equities at June 1995, as shown in Table 9, was at 27.70 times its beginning (December 31, 1975) amount, or slightly more than twice the value of the wealth index for the S&P 500 for the same period.

The recent opening of the Chinese stock market to foreign investors offers investors a potentially exciting investment outlet. The wealth index of Chinese stocks performed poorly during its initial 2½ years, achieving a compound average return in U.S. dollars of –1.67 percent per month, but it is much too early to determine the reliable risk and return characteristics of Chinese equities.

Although direct investment in Korean stocks continues to be restricted, historical performance results for Korea may be of value in the future. After performing roughly in line with the S&P 500 from year-end 1975 to year-end 1985, Korean equities experienced meteoric absolute and relative price increases from 1986 to 1989. The stock values increased more than sixfold, only to relinquish approximately one-half of their cumulative value during the subsequent four years. At the end of June 1995 (see Table 9), US$1.00 invested in Korean stocks at the end of 1975 would have stood at US$21.30, which was substantially above the S&P 500's wealth index at US$13.14.

Philippine stocks have recorded enormous growth since their inclusion in the EMDB at year-end 1984. So great is the price appreciation of Philippine stocks that the wealth index of the S&P 500 over the same time period (US$1.00 to US$3.87) appears flat by comparison (for the Philippines in Table 10, US$1.00 grew to US$40.08). This superior performance was accompanied by significant price variability (see Table 6). For example, Philippine stocks lost more than one-half of their collective market value in 1990 but more than doubled in value in 1992.

Although large gains have occurred in Taiwanese stocks, they have come at the expense of enormous volatility. After spectacular price gains from 1986 to 1989, Taiwanese stocks experienced one of the greatest setbacks ever experienced by a market. In only nine months during 1989, Taiwanese stocks lost almost 80 percent of their combined market value. Nevertheless, as Table 10 reports, at June 30, 1995, the wealth index of Taiwanese stocks for the most recent 10-year period closed at more than 11 times its initial value in U.S. dollars, which was more than double the accumulated value of the wealth index of the S&P 500 over the same time period.

South Asia. India, Indonesia, Malaysia, Pakistan, Sri Lanka, and Thailand are the South Asian emerging markets. As shown in Figure 10, South Asian equities performed in a remarkably similar pattern to U.S. equities during the last half of the 1970s and all of the 1980s. At year-end 1989, the wealth index of South Asian stocks measured in U.S. dollars was at approximately the same level as the wealth index for the S&P 500. The 1990s, however, offered vastly different comparative performance results. In 1991, for example, South Asian equities failed to match the large price increases for U.S. equities; thus, by year-end 1991, the South Asian wealth index had fallen considerably behind the S&P 500. In early 1992, a sudden surge in South Asian stock prices sent the South Asian wealth index temporarily above the S&P 500, but it had fallen below by the end of 1992. Then, in 1993, South Asian stock prices spiked upward, and by year-end 1993, the South Asian wealth index was more than one-third higher than the S&P 500. By June 30, 1995, US$1.00 invested in South Asian stocks at December 31, 1975, stood at US$14.80 (see Table 9), only slightly in excess of the US$13.14 value for the same investment in the S&P 500 over the same time period.

Indian stocks have exhibited wild price gyrations, especially during the most recent decade. For example, Indian stock prices more than doubled during the first half of 1992, relinquished all of those gains and more in the next year, and then more than doubled again in the following year. Table 9 reveals that over the 20-year time period, the wealth index of Indian stocks appreciated to US$18.54, more than the comparable index for the S&P 500 (US$13.14). During the decade ended June 30, 1995, however (see Table 10), Indian stocks underperformed U.S. securities: US$1.00 invested in Indian stocks grew to US$2.68, whereas US$1.00 invested in the S&P 500 appreciated to US$3.87.

Since Indonesia's inclusion in the EMDB at the end of 1989, Indonesian stocks have provided disappointing returns. Table 10 indicates that US$1.00 invested in Indonesian stocks at year-end 1989 would have grown hardly at all (to US$1.03) by mid-1995. Indonesian stocks not only significantly underperformed their U.S. counterparts but also failed to generate returns sufficient to offset U.S. inflation (US$1.43).

Malaysian stock price data extend back to December 1984. During the December 1984–June 1995 period, Malaysian stocks provided approximately the same price appreciation as U.S. stocks. Price variability was especially high in the most recent

Figure 10. Performance of South Asian Emerging Markets versus Various Asset Classes and the CPI, December 1975–June 1995

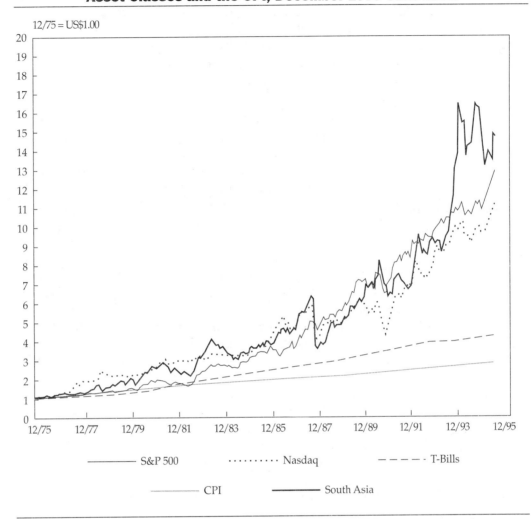

years, as exhibited by the more than doubling of Malaysian stock prices in 1993, followed by wild price gyrations and a sharp price correction in late 1993 and early 1994.

After moving roughly in tandem with the U.S. equity markets from 1985 to 1990, the Pakistani stock market began a series of erratic price movements—more than doubling in 1990, increasing another 50 percent in 1993, and declining almost 75 percent from its peak 1994 value before showing a minor upturn in mid-1985. US$1.00 invested in Pakistani stocks at year-end 1984 appreciated by midyear 1995 (Table 10) to US$5.06, slightly more than US$1.00 invested in the S&P 500 over the same time period (US$3.79).

Data for Sri Lankan stocks date from only year-end 1992. Through midyear 1995, Sri Lankan stocks experienced wild price gyrations but provided returns only slightly in excess of the returns generated by U.S. T-bills. The stock market in Sri Lanka produced a 0.43 percent monthly compound average rate of return from December 1992 to June 1995. T-bills achieved a 0.33 percent monthly compound average rate of return during the same time period. Reliable risk–return characteristics, however, will have to await a longer performance history.

Thai stocks matched the performance of the S&P 500 for 1976 through 1986. After 1986, however, Thai equities began a major upward movement, including almost 100 percent price increases in each of 1989 and 1992. As a result, the wealth index of Thai stocks for the full period (see Table 9) was at US$45.82 on June 30, 1995, more than three times the comparable-period wealth index for the S&P 500 (US$13.14).

Africa. The African emerging markets are Nigeria, South Africa, and Zimbabwe. South Africa was introduced into the EMDB beginning in 1994; thus, pre-1994 results contain only Nigeria and Zimbabwe stock returns. As shown in Figure 11, African stocks performed poorly from 1975 to 1995. US$1.00 invested in African stocks over this time period would be worth only US$0.84 at period end, compared with US$10.01 per dollar invested in the Composite of emerging markets stocks and US$13.14 for a dollar invested in the S&P 500. Thus, Africa was the worst investment outlet, by a substantial margin, among all regions. The 1994 inclusion of the sizable South African market significantly changes the complexion of the African index; thus, past returns may not be very relevant to future performance.

Nigeria. Nigerian stock results begin in 1985. As shown in Table 10, US$1.00 invested in Nigerian stocks at July 1, 1985, would be valued at only US$1.03 after 10 years. Over this time period, Nigerian stocks not only failed to keep up with the U.S.

Figure 11. Performance of African Emerging Markets versus the Various Asset Classes and the CPI, December 1975–June 1995

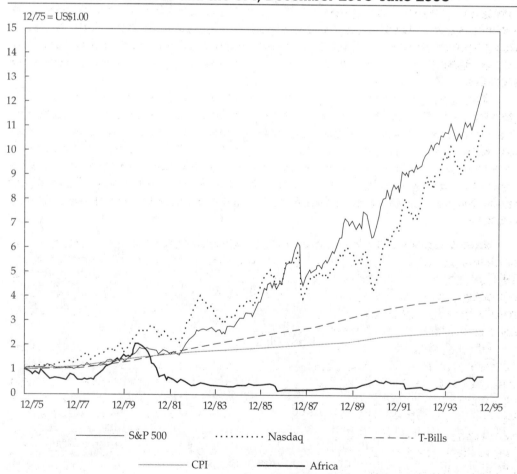

©The Research Foundation of the ICFA

CPI (growth to US$1.43) and T-bills (US$1.78), but they also tied with Indonesia for the lowest appreciation rate among all of the individual emerging markets. Furthermore, the low rates of return have been accompanied by high volatility (see Table 6), including a dramatic Nigerian stock market collapse in early 1995.

■ *South Africa.* Although South African stocks have actively traded for many decades, they were not included in the EMDB until recently, primarily because of South African apartheid policies. Clearly, the addition of South Africa will have substantial repercussions on the African emerging market composite index because of the large size of the market in comparison with other African markets.

■ *Zimbabwe.* Table 9 reveals that US$1.00 invested in Zimbabwean stocks at year-end 1975 had appreciated to US$4.84 at mid-1995, thus providing less than one-half of the value increase of an investment in the S&P 500 (US$13.14) over the same period. After keeping pace with U.S. stocks through 1980, the Zimbabwean market collapsed, losing approximately 80 percent of its value by 1984. Subsequently, Zimbabwean stocks experienced an almost uninterrupted six-year period of explosive growth, moving the wealth index value above the S&P 500 by year-end 1990. During 1991 and 1992, Zimbabwean stocks again lost more than 80 percent of their market value, then rebounded in 1992. The collective results are that the highly volatile Zimbabwean stocks yielded only slightly better returns than low-risk U.S. T-bills from 1975 to 1995.

Variations in Performance over Five-Year Periods

The preceding discussions clearly show that over the 20-year period of our data, emerging markets have gone through periods of extremes in performance. The variations across time should serve to remind the investor of the boilerplate caveat that goes on virtually all mutual fund reports of performance: "Past performance may not be indicative of future performance." The warning goes double in emerging markets.

Why does performance vary so much in these markets? A key reason is that governments change fundamental economic policies, and in the case of emerging markets, those policies can have dramatic effects on security values. This section provides details of the extent to which emerging markets have registered variations in performance over time by breaking down the performance for the nine markets that have been in the EMDB for the full period into five-year segments. The final part of the chapter then illustrates the effects of important economic events in particular markets.

Nine Markets with 20 Years of Data: Wealth Appreciation. Variations in performance for the nine markets that have been in the IFC's EMDB since December 1975 are shown in the five-year segments of data given in Table 12. The data are the compound values of a US$1.00 investment in each of the markets. The wealth index results in Table 12 reinforce the earlier demonstration that the emerging markets have widely varying performance even over relatively long periods.

Of these nine markets, Chile is the most extreme example. On the one hand, an investor putting US$1.00 in a value-weighted portfolio in the Chilean market at the end of December 1975 would have had US$33.40 by the end of the June 1980, a gain of 3,340 percent. On the other hand, if the investor had put US$1.00 in the market at the end of June 1980, the investor would have had only US$0.16 five years later—a performance consistent with a –84 percent return. This 1980–85 period spanned the beginning of the Latin American debt crisis. The same investor entering the market in Chile at the end of June 1985 would have seen the US$1.00 grow by a factor of 10

Table 12. Five-Year Compound Values of a US$1.00 Investment in Markets Listed in the EMDB from December 1975

Market	12/75–6/80	6/80–6/85	6/85–6/90	6/90–6/95
Argentina	29.42	0.19	6.21	3.93
Brazil	0.83	1.81	1.11	3.04
Chile	33.40	0.16	10.04	6.25
Greece	1.00	0.25	12.33	0.55
India	2.59	2.68	1.45	1.85
Korea	2.91	0.99	5.96	1.24
Mexico	3.45	0.33	9.98	1.69
Thailand	2.07	1.48	6.61	2.26
Zimbabwe	1.59	0.63	5.48	0.89

Note: The values shown are compound values of a US$1.00 investment at the start of the period listed at the top of each column and held until the end of the period listed at the top of the column. The only markets included are those for which data were available for the entire time period of our study, December 1975 to June 1995.

times in the subsequent five years.

Timing is everything, but unfortunately, the correct timing is not easy to see before the fact. Argentina's five-year compound growth values were nearly as volatile as Chile's, but Chile's returns after June 1985 were substantially greater than Argentina's. This outcome may be associated with the fact that Chile's reform process led that of Argentina by nearly a decade. The results for Chile and Argentina during the second period in Table 12 are similar to the results for a U.S. investor who entered the U.S. market just before the Great Depression. Such an investor would have lost about 80 percent of her or his investment in large stocks or about 90 percent in small stocks. Thus, the terrible performance of these two Latin American markets in the 1980–85 period is not without precedent elsewhere.

Among the nine markets in Table 12, the ones with the least volatile five-year performances are India and Brazil. India's relative stability is not surprising; Table 6 showed that India's monthly standard deviation of returns has been among the lowest in the EMDB. Brazil, however, had a monthly standard deviation that ranked second only to Argentina (in Table 6), yet its successive five-year returns are relatively stable. It is as if Brazil has a high degree of volatility around a constant central tendency; over five-year periods, the dominant effect has been the central tendency.

Figure 12 demonstrates graphically the successive five-year compound values for the nine markets. The contrast between the large variations in performance for Argentina and Chile and the comparative stability of India and Brazil stands out clearly. Stability is presumably a good thing, but note that the impression of instability for Argentina and Chile in Figure 12 is caused primarily by the extremely *high* performance in the earliest period. Of course, as noted, no markets fell so far in the second period. Not only did Argentina and Chile fail to continue their prior high performance, but each lost more than 80 percent of its value.

Figure 12. Successive Five-Year Compound Growth for Nine Markets

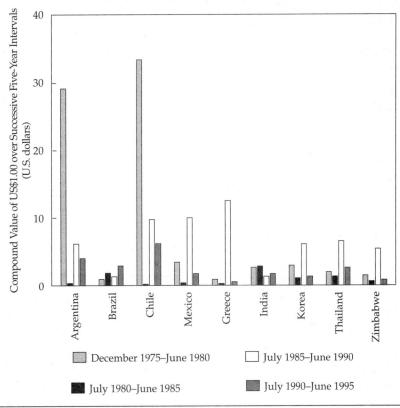

December 1975–June 1980 ☐ July 1985–June 1990

July 1980–June 1985 July 1990–June 1995

Note: Includes only those companies entering the database as of December 1975.

Risk and Return for Five-Year Periods: All EMDB Markets. Tables 13–16 provide compound values of a US$1.00 investment and an investment of one unit of local currency in successive five-year periods for all the markets in the EMDB as of the middle of 1995. As previously, if a market was included in the EMDB before the end of the five-year period relevant to the table, that market is included in the table with results based on the portion of the period for which data were available. (Beginning dates for a market's inclusion in the EMDB are given in Table 1.) For comparison, results are also shown for the S&P 500, the Nasdaq, T-bills, and the U.S. CPI.

Note from Tables 13–16 that the Composite gained 227 percent in the first five-year period, lost 49 percent of its value in the next period, gained 262 percent in the subsequent period, and gained 66 percent in the final five-year period. The average emerging market currency lost value in each of the periods, which is reflected by the fact that compound values of the Composite in local currency terms are greater in each of the periods than are values in U.S. dollar terms. Of course, as discussed previously, some emerging market currencies gained against the dollar in some time periods. During the December 1975 to June 1980 period, for example, Jordan and India registered higher compound changes in dollar terms than in local currency terms. In each of the subperiods, at least one of the emerging markets experienced lower compound growth in local currency terms than in U.S. dollar terms. Especially noteworthy are some of the Asian markets in the latter half of the 1980s and in the first half of the 1990s.

Table 13. Compound Values as of June 1980 Based on All Data Available December 1975–June 1980

Market	US$1.00 Invested	1 Unit of Local Currency Invested
Composite	3.27	4.54
S&P 500	1.58	—
Nasdaq	2.03	—
T-bills	1.39	—
CPI	1.49	—
EMA	1.30	1.46
Europe	1.00	1.22
Greece	1.00	1.22
Jordan	2.37	2.21
Africa	1.59	1.61
Zimbabwe	1.59	1.61
Latin America	5.99	14.13
Argentina	29.42	84.97
Brazil	0.83	4.86
Chile	33.40	153.27
Mexico	3.45	6.32
Asia	2.47	2.60
East Asia	2.91	3.63
Korea	2.91	3.63
South Asia	2.26	2.09
India	2.59	2.26
Thailand	2.07	2.07

Note: Data had to start before June 1980 to be included in this table.

Table 14. Compound Values as of June 1985 Based on All Data Available June 1980–June 1985

Market	US$1.00 Invested	1 Unit of Local Currency Invested
Composite	0.51	1.22
S&P 500	2.15	—
Nasdaq	1.88	—
T-bills	1.71	—
CPI	1.30	—
EMA	0.62	1.22
Europe	0.25	0.79
Greece	0.25	0.79
Jordan	1.53	2.07
Africa	0.25	0.65
Nigeria	1.01	1.12
Zimbabwe	0.63	1.55
Latin America	0.25	1.46
Argentina	0.19	610.92
Brazil	1.81	202.17
Chile	0.16	0.63
Colombia	0.93	1.17
Mexico	0.33	20.79
Venezuela	1.17	1.17
Asia	1.37	2.05
East Asia	2.76	4.83
Korea	0.99	1.44
Philippines	1.23	1.15
Taiwan	0.74	0.76
South Asia	1.58	2.45
India	2.68	4.27
Malaysia	0.99	1.01
Pakistan	1.11	1.16
Thailand	1.48	1.99

Note: Data had to start before June 1985 to be included in this table.

Table 15. Compound Values as of June 1990 Based on All Data Available June 1985–June 1990

Market	US$1.00 Invested	1 Unit of Local Currency Invested
Composite	3.62	5.04
S&P 500	2.22	—
Nasdaq	1.56	—
T-bills	1.41	—
CPI	1.21	—
EMA	3.99	8.61
Europe	13.49	18.48
Greece	12.33	14.76
Portugal	7.89	7.19
Turkey	14.45	1.29
Jordan	1.14	1.89
Africa	1.19	7.35
Nigeria	0.67	5.90
Zimbabwe	5.48	8.66
Latin America	7.37	87.03
Argentina	6.21	33,107.21
Brazil	1.11	11,141.46
Chile	10.04	18.32
Colombia	6.10	20.70
Mexico	9.98	124.66
Venezuela	1.55	9.72
Asia	3.29	2.96
East Asia	8.63	6.53
Korea	5.96	4.81
Philippines	15.94	19.40
Taiwan	9.58	6.52
South Asia	2.01	2.32
India	1.45	2.02
Indonesia	1.40	1.44
Malaysia	1.89	2.05
Pakistan	1.72	2.33
Thailand	6.61	6.20

Note: Data had to start before June 1990 to be included in this table.

Table 16. Compound Values as of June 1995 Based on All Data Available June 1990–June 1995

Market	US$1.00 Invested	1 Unit of Local Currency Invested
Composite	1.66	3.85
		—
S&P 500	1.75	—
Nasdaq	2.02	—
T-bills	1.26	—
CPI	1.19	—
EMA	1.01	2.25
Europe	0.70	2.31
Greece	0.55	0.77
Hungary	1.05	1.56
Poland	4.99	8.02
Portugal	1.09	1.12
Turkey	0.55	1.09
Jordan	1.63	1.70
Africa	1.79	5.14
Nigeria	1.53	16.24
South Africa	1.43	1.18
Zimbabwe	0.89	3.06
Latin America	3.24	42.95
Argentina	3.93	7.34
Brazil	3.04	128,543.87
Chile	6.25	8.19
Colombia	6.86	14.39
Mexico	1.69	3.70
Peru	2.20	3.00
Venezuela	1.66	5.97
Asia	1.45	1.52
East Asia	1.16	1.17
China	0.60	0.63
Korea	1.24	1.33
Philippines	2.51	2.86
Taiwan	1.16	1.10
South Asia	2.01	2.26
India	1.85	3.34
Indonesia	0.74	0.85
Malaysia	2.26	2.04
Pakistan	2.94	4.20
Sri Lanka	1.14	1.24
Thailand	2.26	2.17

A highlight of Table 15 is the extraordinary gains of Argentina and Brazil in local currency terms vis-à-vis U.S. dollar terms during the 1985–90 period. Argentina registered a full 521 percent gain in value in U.S. dollar terms in that period, in spite of suffering huge currency depreciation against the dollar. Note that Argentina's enormous percentage gain in U.S. dollar terms occurred in the same period in which the Nasdaq gained only 56 percent and the S&P 500 only 122 percent. Thus, a stable currency is not a necessary condition for strong investment performance.[4] The same

---

[4]Some evidence exists that, within limits, a weak currency is associated with increasing share prices because exporters with high domestic content in their products benefit from lower relative costs. Dramatic losses in currency values do tend to be associated, however, with unstable economic conditions.

phenomenon is illustrated in Table 16: Brazil in the 1990–95 period registered a local currency gain of 12,854,287 percent (related to a series of huge inflationary periods) while it gained 204 percent in U.S. dollar terms. During the same period, the S&P 500 and Nasdaq gained, respectively, only 75 percent and 102 percent.

Tables 17–20 show mean monthly returns and standard deviations of monthly returns for the successive five-year periods. Note that in the first three periods (Tables 17, 18, and 19), Argentina registered the highest standard deviation of the markets, but it fell to fifth place (in U.S. dollar terms) during the final, 1990–95, period (Table 20) when Poland and China were added to the EMDB and Turkey and Nigeria registered high volatility. As a rule, Latin American markets have typically been more volatile than others, but their volatility has become relatively less pronounced in recent years. Moreover, new markets that come onto the global scene tend to experience volatile periods early in their emergence.

Table 17. Monthly Mean Returns, Standard Deviations, and Compound Average Returns: All Data Available December 1975–June 1980

Market	U.S. Dollar			Local Currency		
	Arithmetic Average Return	Standard Deviation	Compound Average Return	Arithmetic Average Return	Standard Deviation	Compound Average Return
Composite	2.30%	4.12%	2.22%	2.90%	3.48%	2.84%
EMA	0.58	4.25	0.49	0.77	3.78	0.70
Europe	0.12	4.78	0.01	0.45	4.14	0.36
Greece	0.12	4.78	0.01	0.45	4.14	0.36
Jordan	3.21	6.52	3.02	2.97	6.60	2.78
Africa	1.23	8.84	0.86	1.24	8.58	0.89
Zimbabwe	1.23	8.84	0.86	1.24	8.58	0.89
Latin America	3.74	8.74	3.37	5.25	6.98	5.03
Argentina	10.78	32.33	6.46	14.22	36.62	8.57
Brazil	0.15	10.02	−0.33	3.43	.92	2.97
Chile	7.73	15.41	6.71	10.67	14.79	9.77
Mexico	2.84	10.05	2.32	3.75	7.59	3.47
Asia	1.82	5.15	1.69	1.90	4.86	1.79
East Asia	2.47	10.29	2.00	2.87	10.18	2.41
Korea	2.47	10.29	2.00	2.87	10.18	2.41
South Asia	1.62	4.57	1.52	1.45	4.07	1.37
India	1.89	4.80	1.78	1.61	4.24	1.52
Thailand	1.62	7.59	1.36	1.62	7.57	1.36

Table 18. Monthly Mean Returns, Standard Deviations, and Compound Average Returns: All Data Available June 1980–June 1985

Market	U.S. Dollar			Local Currency		
	Arithmetic Average Return	Standard Deviation	Compound Average Return	Arithmetic Average Return	Standard Deviation	Compound Average Return
Composite	−1.05%	3.59%	−1.11%	0.40%	3.80%	0.33%
EMA	−0.70	4.44	−0.80	0.40	3.87	0.33
Europe	−2.07	6.40	−2.27	−0.24	5.66	−0.39
Greece	−2.07	6.40	−2.27	−0.24	5.66	−0.39
Jordan	0.83	5.17	0.71	1.33	4.85	1.22
Africa	−1.69	10.87	−2.30	−0.14	10.66	−0.72
Zimbabwe	0.08	13.28	−0.77	1.55	13.15	0.73
Latin America	−2.00	7.90	−2.31	0.95	8.15	0.63
Argentina	0.66	30.63	−2.77	15.13	33.28	11.28
Brazil	2.00	14.80	1.00	10.37	16.28	9.25
Chile	−2.61	9.06	−3.03	−0.33	9.15	−0.76
Colombia	−1.19	1.99	−1.20	2.61	1.63	2.60
Mexico	−0.91	12.99	−1.83	2.60	11.29	2.00
Venezuela	2.66	0.95	2.66	2.66	0.95	2.66
Asia	0.60	4.01	0.52	1.28	4.00	1.20
East Asia	0.25	8.58	−0.09	0.82	8.61	0.48
Korea	0.34	8.63	−0.01	0.95	8.64	0.61
Taiwan	−2.74	1.18	−2.74	−2.51	1.47	−2.52
South Asia	0.89	3.89	0.81	1.62	3.72	1.56
India	1.82	6.01	1.65	2.60	5.64	2.45
Malaysia	−0.17	4.17	−0.24	0.28	4.32	0.20
Pakistan	1.79	3.08	1.75	2.47	2.45	2.44
Thailand	0.76	4.57	0.66	1.23	4.09	1.15

Table 19. Monthly Mean Returns, Standards Deviations, and Compound Average Returns: All Data Available June 1985–June 1990

Market	U.S. Dollar			Local Currency		
	Arithmetic Average Return	Standard Deviation	Compound Average Return	Arithmetic Average Return	Standard Deviation	Compound Average Return
Composite	2.45%	7.48%	2.17%	3.03%	7.61%	2.73%
EMA	2.79	9.97	2.33	4.07	9.54	3.65
Europe	5.20	13.05	4.43	5.71	12.70	4.98
Greece	5.26	15.03	4.28	5.49	14.48	4.59
Portugal	5.14	16.92	3.90	4.99	17.04	3.72
Turkey	9.04	24.46	6.56	12.19	24.64	0.60
Jordan	0.34	5.16	0.21	1.20	5.19	1.07
Africa	0.80	9.08	0.30	3.43	3.09	3.38
Nigeria	0.13	11.43	−0.66	3.08	4.16	3.00
Zimbabwe	3.04	5.94	2.87	3.79	5.25	3.66
Latin America	3.97	10.50	3.38	8.31	10.88	7.73
Argentina	8.01	36.97	3.09	27.92	61.18	18.94
Brazil	3.74	27.59	0.17	22.46	44.04	16.80
Chile	4.24	8.13	3.92	5.26	7.91	4.97
Colombia	3.25	6.41	3.06	5.36	6.23	5.18
Mexico	5.43	16.15	3.91	9.72	16.34	8.37
Venezuela	1.70	13.52	0.73	4.35	10.29	3.86
Asia	2.33	7.94	2.01	2.14	7.85	1.83
East Asia	4.21	10.55	3.66	3.71	10.35	3.18
Korea	3.41	9.03	3.02	3.03	8.91	2.65
Philippines	5.32	11.45	4.72	5.72	12.25	5.07
Taiwan	5.17	16.64	3.84	4.45	16.23	3.17
South Asia	1.35	5.86	1.17	1.59	5.88	1.41
India	0.95	8.19	0.62	1.51	8.23	1.18
Indonesia	6.11	9.67	5.74	6.56	9.54	6.21
Malaysia	1.43	8.44	1.06	1.56	8.31	1.21
Pakistan	0.95	3.07	0.91	1.46	2.93	1.42
Thailand	3.55	8.24	3.20	3.44	8.23	3.09

Table 20. Monthly Mean Returns, Standard Deviations, and Compound Average Returns: All Data Available June 1990–June 1995

Market	U.S. Dollar			Local Currency		
	Arithmetic Average Return	Standard Deviation	Compound Average Return	Arithmetic Average Return	Standard Deviation	Compound Average Return
Composite	1.00%	5.66%	0.84%	2.44%	5.87%	2.27%
EMA	0.31	7.73	0.01	1.62	7.37	1.36
Europe	–0.21	9.03	–0.60	1.77	8.74	1.41
Greece	–0.62	8.63	–0.98	–0.06	9.02	–0.44
Hungary	1.02	14.67	0.18	2.38	15.00	1.50
Poland	8.13	25.70	5.51	10.08	27.19	7.19
Portugal	0.34	6.48	0.14	0.35	5.67	0.20
Turkey	0.52	17.88	–0.99	5.05	16.77	0.15
Jordan	0.92	4.60	0.81	0.99	4.50	0.89
Africa	1.52	10.65	0.97	2.89	5.10	2.77
Nigeria	2.81	19.95	0.71	4.84	4.37	4.76
South Africa	2.40	7.34	2.14	1.13	5.20	0.99
Zimbabwe	0.34	10.45	–0.20	2.39	10.20	1.88
Latin America	2.25	7.48	1.98	6.75	7.79	6.47
Argentina	3.51	17.58	2.11	4.81	19.33	10.45
Brazil	3.12	16.52	1.87	24.04	25.00	21.66
Chile	3.41	8.05	3.10	3.84	7.55	3.57
Colombia	3.83	11.35	3.26	5.14	11.69	4.54
Mexico	1.50	10.82	0.87	2.59	8.92	2.20
Peru	3.57	13.74	2.67	4.64	13.92	3.73
Venezuela	1.71	13.52	0.85	3.85	13.37	3.02
Asia	0.84	6.63	0.62	0.92	6.70	0.70
East Asia	0.59	8.31	0.25	0.60	8.21	0.27
China	0.47	23.99	–1.67	0.54	23.56	–1.52
Korea	0.64	7.87	0.35	0.76	7.81	0.47
Philippines	2.03	10.02	1.55	2.25	10.08	1.77
Taiwan	1.05	13.17	0.25	0.96	13.11	0.16
South Asia	1.37	6.48	1.17	1.58	6.70	1.37
India	1.59	10.96	1.03	2.70	12.12	2.03
Indonesia	–0.13	8.69	–0.50	0.10	8.66	–0.27
Malaysia	1.65	7.52	1.37	1.49	7.79	1.19
Pakistan	2.23	9.57	1.82	2.85	9.71	2.42
Sri Lanka	0.89	9.83	0.43	1.18	9.82	0.72
Thailand	1.83	9.85	1.37	1.77	9.99	1.30

Economic Policies and Market Performance

The policy changes and their effects in this section were chosen to illustrate the importance of following economic events in emerging markets that the reader is considering for investment. All of the figures in this section are based on market indexes expressed in U.S. dollar terms.

Argentina. The effects of the enactment of the Convertibility Plan in Argentina in early 1991 and the initial public offering (IPO) of YPF in June 1993 are depicted in Figure 13. The Convertibility Plan was the brainchild of Domingo Cavallo, the former Argentine Minister of the Economy and the man credited with having stabilized Argentina's economy. Under the Convertibility Plan, Argentina pegs the value of the peso (initially, 10,000 australs) one-to-one with the U.S. dollar. In addition, the government maintains a policy of limiting money creation to the amount of foreign

Figure 13. Economic Policy Changes and Market Performance: Argentina, December 1975–June 1995

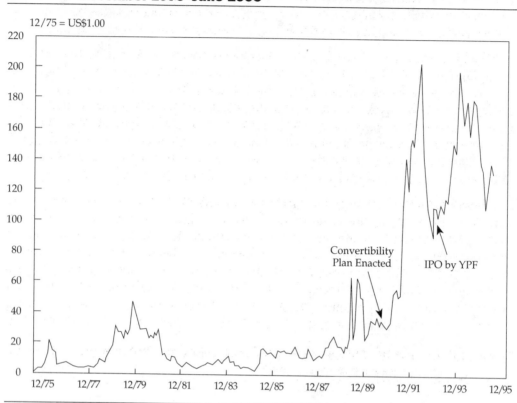

reserves on hand, thus guaranteeing convertibility of any amount of Argentine currency at any time. In essence, the Convertibility Plan removed monetary policy from the discretion of the government. In response to implementation of the plan, inflation quickly fell, interest rates began a sharp decline, and capital flight was reversed. The Argentine equity market increased by some 400 percent (in U.S. dollar terms) during the remainder of 1991.

The second event highlighted in Figure 13 is the initial public offering of YPF, the former national petroleum company of Argentina. YPF was notable for its inefficiency and, despite its near-monopoly position in the petroleum markets of Argentina, chronic losses. Although focusing on a single initial public offering as a key economic event might at first glance seem odd, the privatization of national assets has been a major step in the liberalizing of emerging market economies. Moreover, YPF is the largest security (measured by market capitalization and by trading) on the Argentine Bolsa. Its privatization was one of a series of moves by the government of Carlos Menem to privatize national assets. In fact, three stocks on the Argentine Bolsa account for more than 50 percent of the market capitalization of the full market: YPF and the two telephone companies that were created from the former national telephone company. YPF's initial public offering was followed by another rapid run up in security prices that ended only with the collapse of the Mexican peso in December 1994.

Mexico. The devastating effect of the devaluation of the Mexican peso that occurred on December 19, 1994, is clearly visible in Figure 14. Earlier peso devaluations in 1976 and 1982 are associated with other declines in the value of the

Mexican market, but no effect is so sharp as the one in 1994. Figure 14 also shows the effect of Mexico's August 1982 closing of its foreign exchange markets. In response to rapid capital flight, the country imposed restrictions on the conversion of the domestic currency and froze the foreign currency accounts of its citizens.

Turkey. As Figure 15 shows, Turkey has historically had a volatile market. The event singled out is the downgrading of Turkey's sovereign debt by Moody's (from investment grade to speculative grade) in January 1994. Investors feared a severe devaluation of the Turkish lira, which indeed materialized, and expected a new austerity program. A body of research in the United States demonstrates that the downgrading of U.S. corporate debt often follows rather than leads the decline in value of a corporation's equity. In Turkey, the downgrade was itself apparently newsworthy to the market and was associated with a sharp decline in the equity market.

South Korea. A warning about government announcements versus government actions is provided by the case of South Korea. Since the early 1980s, Korea's government has often made announcements about the opening up of its capital markets to foreign ownership. Figure 16 points out the effects of several such moves. In January 1981, the government announced a plan to internationalize the capital market. This move was followed by years of promised additional opening—and failures to achieve such opening. One particularly newsworthy move was the creation of the well-known Korea Fund (a closed-end fund) in August 1984. Finally, during late

Figure 14. Economic Policy Changes and Market Performance: Mexico, December 1975–June 1995

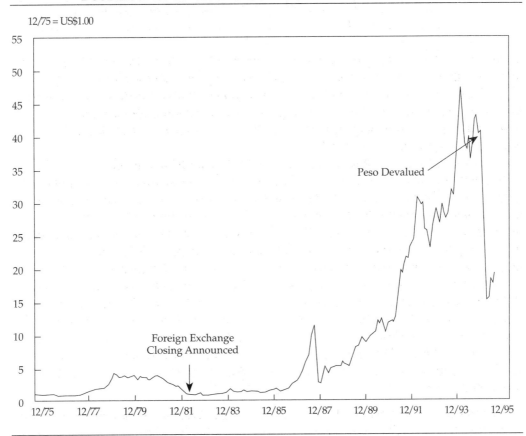

1991 through January 1992, a series of announcements were made permitting foreign investment in significant percentages of the equity in Korean stocks. What is noteworthy from Figure 16 is that these announcements do not appear to be associated with the market performance one might expect from such a market opening. Thus, investors would be well advised not to assume that announced intentions to open a market will be greeted with increases in the value of the shares in that market.

Conclusion

The comprehensive data and discussion in this chapter of the rates of return and risks of emerging markets—in the aggregate, by regions, and for individual country markets—was designed to equip the investor with solid empirical information about the long-term performance of securities in emerging markets. The chapter illustrated the high variability in the performance of emerging markets over time. Whether measured in monthly standard deviations or in five-year compound growth, emerging markets have been highly inconsistent in performance over time. Thus, investors should be aware that not only do emerging markets entail high risk but the risk is not necessarily removed by commitment to a "long" holding period. Furthermore, the higher risk, or greater variability in returns, is not always compensated with higher returns. Finally, currency considerations can dramatically affect the performance analysis of a given market and must be seriously considered in portfolio design.

Figure 15. Economic Policy Changes and Market Performance: Turkey, December 1986–June 1995

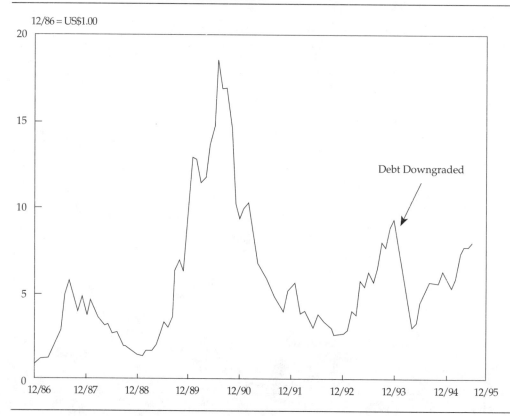

©The Research Foundation of the ICFA

Figure 16. Economic Policy Changes and Market Performance: Korea, December 1975–June 1995

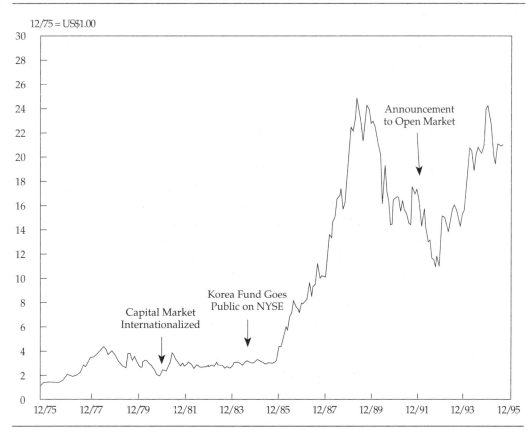

2. Portfolio Construction Using Emerging Markets

One of the key concepts of modern portfolio theory (MPT) is the efficient portfolio—a portfolio that combines assets so as to minimize the risk for a given level of return. In order to evaluate the efficiency of various portfolio combinations, the investor must know the expected return and risk characteristics of each of the individual securities within the portfolio. In addition, to determine the overall return and risk characteristics of the portfolio, the investor must understand how the securities interact.

Correlation Statistics

In Chapter 1, we focused on the returns and risks of the emerging markets as a class, emerging markets grouped by geographical regions, and emerging country markets. In this section, we address the relationships between the returns of the various countries and regions. For this purpose, we calculated the standard deviation of returns as the measure of portfolio risk. For a multiasset portfolio, the standard deviation is expressed as follows:

$$\sigma_{portfolio} = (\Sigma_i \Sigma_j w_i w_j \rho_{ij} \sigma_i \sigma_j)^{1/2},$$

where

σ = standard deviation

Σ = the sum over all of the investments in the portfolio (i = 1, 2, 3, ..., N)

w = the weight of an investment in the portfolio

ρ_{ij} = the correlation between investment i and investment j

The correlation coefficient, ρ, measures the degree of association between pairs of investments in the portfolio. Although a correlation coefficient can range in value from –1 to +1, in most cases, its value falls somewhere in between these two extremes.

Whenever two assets have a correlation coefficient less than 1.0, some risk reduction will occur when the two assets are combined in a portfolio—that is, the portfolio's risk will be less than the weighted-average risk of the individual securities. The lower the correlation between the assets, the greater will be the risk reduction. In fact, when two assets are negatively correlated, the combination of the two assets can produce a portfolio with a lower standard deviation of returns than that for either of the two assets alone. Consequently, the most important risk consideration for an individual asset may not be its own risk level but how it contributes to total portfolio risk through its correlation with the other assets in the portfolio.

Correlations with U.S. Markets. One of the benefits of investing in emerging markets is that the security returns in these markets are not highly correlated with the returns of the developed markets. Therefore, adding emerging market securities to portfolios containing only securities from developed markets can reduce overall portfolio risk, even though securities from emerging markets are characterized by higher expected risk than securities from developed markets.

Table 21 shows that in the full 1975–95 period, the returns from portfolios of the emerging markets typically had low or negative correlations with U.S. stocks—the S&P 500 Index and the National Association of Securities Dealers Automated Quotation Composite Index (Nasdaq). During this period, our Emerging Markets Composite Value-Weighted Index (the Composite) had only a 0.27 correlation with the S&P 500 (0.28 with the Nasdaq).

Table 21. Correlations between Emerging Markets and U.S. Equity Markets

Market	December 1975–June 1995[a]		June 1985–June 1990[b]		June 1985–June 1995[b]		June 1990–June 1995[c]	
	S&P 500	Nasdaq	S&P 500	Nasdaq	S&P 500	Nasdaq	S&P 500	Nasdaq
Composite	0.27	0.28	0.31	0.32	0.34	0.35	0.41	0.42
EMA	0.11	0.06	0.11	0.12	0.12	0.08	0.12	0.05
Europe	0.10	0.05	0.12	0.10	0.13	0.08	0.12	0.07
Greece	0.10	0.08	0.07	0.07	0.14	0.12	0.29	0.27
Hungary	na	na	na	na	na	na	0.35	0.31
Poland	na	na	na	na	na	na	0.28	0.43
Portugal	na	na	0.17	0.14	0.22	0.15	0.43	0.27
Turkey	na	na	0.07	0.05	0.01	−0.05	−0.12	−0.15
Jordan	0.08	0.06	−0.06	−0.08	0.04	0.07	0.23	0.26
Africa	0.07	0.06	0.06	0.08	0.04	0.05	0.03	0.02
Nigeria	0.02	0.05	0.10	0.12	0.03	0.05	−0.02	0.01
South Africa	na	na	na	na	na	na	0.26	0.24
Zimbabwe	0.03	0.01	−0.30	−0.26	−0.10	−0.11	0.03	−0.02
Latin America	0.24	0.26	0.41	0.41	0.41	0.41	0.38	0.42
Argentina	0.03	0.05	−0.02	0.02	0.06	0.10	0.30	0.31
Brazil	0.05	0.06	−0.03	0.03	0.10	0.15	0.43	0.39
Chile	0.04	0.07	0.26	0.30	0.29	0.33	0.36	0.37
Colombia	0.08	0.12	0.12	0.11	0.09	0.14	0.10	0.17
Mexico	0.28	0.28	0.45	0.39	0.39	0.36	0.24	0.33
Peru	na	na	na	na	na	na	0.12	0.39
Venezuela	−0.04	−0.03	0.00	0.05	−0.05	−0.03	−0.12	−0.12
Asia	0.21	0.22	0.24	0.26	0.27	0.28	0.32	0.32
East Asia	0.16	0.16	0.18	0.20	0.21	0.21	0.27	0.26
China	na	na	na	na	na	na	0.06	0.08
Korea	0.16	0.16	0.31	0.27	0.23	0.20	0.06	0.14
Philippines	0.25	0.22	0.16	0.10	0.24	0.21	0.38	0.37
Taiwan	0.14	0.14	0.08	0.11	0.15	0.15	0.28	0.22
South Asia	0.24	0.24	0.52	0.52	0.38	0.39	0.23	0.26
India	−0.01	0.01	0.02	0.06	−0.06	−0.04	−0.16	−0.14
Indonesia	na	na	−0.15	−0.11	0.26	0.25	0.34	0.32
Malaysia	0.45	0.41	0.54	0.50	0.46	0.42	0.33	0.32
Pakistan	−0.02	0.00	−0.12	−0.04	−0.02	0.00	0.04	0.01
Sri Lanka	na	na	na	na	na	na	−0.12	0.03
Thailand	0.15	0.17	0.37	0.41	0.33	0.38	0.31	0.37

na = not applicable.

[a]Data had to start before July 1985 to be included in this time series.

[b]Data had to start before July 1990 to be included in these time series.

[c]Price data for Hungary, Poland, Peru, China, and Sri Lanka start on December 1992. Price data for South Africa start in January 1994.

Note: Correlations calculated using all available U.S. dollar returns over the indicated periods.

Among the several regional groups, Latin America had the highest correlation with the United States (0.24 for the S&P 500 and 0.26 for the Nasdaq) for the total time period, although it was only slightly greater than the correlation of the U.S. market with Asia (0.21 and 0.22). The relationship of the U.S. stock market with the European and African markets was substantially weaker; the Europe index had a correlation of only 0.10 with the S&P 500 (0.05 with the Nasdaq), and the Africa index had a correlation of 0.07 with the S&P 500 (0.06 with the Nasdaq). Of special interest is the fact that the Latin American and Asian markets have become more closely related to the U.S. markets during recent years, whereas the returns of European and African stocks continue to have virtually no relationship to U.S. stock market returns.

Only Malaysia among the 16 emerging markets for which data were available for the full time period had a meaningfully high correlation with the U.S. markets (0.45 with the S&P 500 and 0.41 with the Nasdaq). Because Malaysia is among the largest and is, arguably, one of the most economically developed of the emerging markets, it is not surprising that Malaysia's equity markets would have the highest correlation with U.S. stocks.

With a 0.28 correlation coefficient between it and both the S&P 500 and the Nasdaq, the Mexican stock market had the next closest relationship to the U.S. markets. This relationship would be expected because of the relatively large size of the Mexican stock market and the country's geographical proximity to the United States. The correlation has varied across subperiods, registering a high of 0.45 with the S&P 500 in the 1985–90 period versus only 0.24 for the 1990–95 period.

Over the entire data period, the equity returns for three emerging markets were negatively correlated with the S&P 500 (Venezuela at –0.04, Pakistan at –0.02, and India at –0.01). These markets continue to be negatively or only slightly positively correlated with the U.S. markets, as shown by their correlation coefficients for the 1985–95 and 1990–95 periods. Zimbabwe was the only other emerging market to be negatively correlated (–0.10) with the U.S. market from 1985 through 1995, and in the 1990–95 period, the negative correlation declined to –0.03.

Several major changes have occurred over time in the correlations between various emerging markets and the U.S. market. For example, as Table 21 shows, the correlation coefficient between the Chilean stock market and the S&P 500 was only 0.04 for the entire 1975–95 period, indicating that stock market returns between these two markets were almost randomly related. The Chilean economy has developed substantially in recent years, however, with the result that the Chilean and U.S. stock markets have become much more related. The correlation between these two markets increased to 0.29 for the most recent 10-year period and to 0.36 for the most recent 5-year period.

The same phenomenon occurred between the S&P 500 and Brazilian stocks, as evidenced by an increase in the correlation between these markets from 0.05 for the full 1976–95 period to 0.43 for the 1990–95 period. The Brazilian market also shows how volatile the relationship of emerging markets to the U.S. markets can be. As recently as the 1985–90 period, the S&P 500 and Brazilian stocks were slightly negatively correlated.

Among the Asian markets, several noticeable changes occurred in various periods. Taiwan, the largest emerging market in terms of market capitalization, experienced a significant correlation increase with the United States. Over the 1975–95 period (see Table 21), the correlation coefficient was 0.14 with both the S&P 500 and the Nasdaq; for the 1990–95 period, however, the correlation was 0.28 with the S&P 500 (0.22 with the Nasdaq). Thailand, the sixth largest emerging market, experienced a similar change; its correlation with the S&P 500 was only 0.15 (0.17 with the Nasdaq) for the full period but was 0.31 (0.37) for the 1990–95 period. Two other large Asian markets, Korea and Malaysia, showed declines in their correlation coefficients with the U.S. markets between the full period and the two most recent five-year periods (1985–90 versus 1990–95).

Correlations between Emerging Markets. Empirical research has also revealed that, in addition to low correlations with developed markets, such as the U.S. markets, equity portfolios from the various emerging markets are not highly correlated among themselves. Correlation coefficients for all pairs of regional markets and for all pairs of emerging markets are presented in Table 22. Generally, the correlations between the emerging country markets are low, even for stock markets within the same geographical region. For example, only the Peruvian stock market showed any significant relationship with other Latin American markets (0.57 correlation with Chile and 0.47 with Argentina and Mexico); none of the other pairs of Latin American markets had correlations of more than 0.25. Some of the relationships were especially weak, such as the –0.03 correlation between neighbors Brazil and Venezuela.

The correlations between pairs of Asian markets are somewhat larger than those between pairs of Latin American markets. The highest correlation of returns shown in Table 22 is between Malaysia and Thailand, which are among the large emerging markets. The two largest East Asian markets, however, Taiwan and Korea, had a correlation coefficient of only 0.07, indicating virtually no relationship.

Efficient Frontiers Combining U.S. and Emerging Markets. Figure 17 contains the risk–return curve for portfolios containing various combinations of emerging markets and S&P 500 stocks for the December 1975–June 1995 period. As shown, a portfolio composed entirely of emerging market stocks was inefficient—that is, it experienced lower returns at higher risk in this period than did a portfolio consisting entirely of U.S. stocks. Nevertheless, some efficient portfolios did contain emerging market stocks because of the diversification benefits provided by emerging markets. Portfolios containing 30 percent or less of emerging market stocks fell on the efficient portion of the risk–return curve, the efficient frontier.

For the most recent decade, emerging market securities experienced much stronger relative returns. Consequently, as illustrated in Figure 18, the efficient frontier for this period includes a greater representation of emerging market stocks. Portfolios ranging from 20 percent to 100 percent investment in emerging markets fell on the efficient frontier. A particularly important result is that a portfolio mix of 20 percent emerging market stocks represented the lowest risk portfolio on the efficient frontier. Thus, the addition of the higher risk emerging market securities created a portfolio less risky than a portfolio composed entirely of U.S. stocks—a prime example of the beneficial reduction of overall portfolio risk by adding nondomestic securities having low correlations with domestic securities. The diversification benefit is so powerful that a portfolio containing only U.S. stocks is dominated by portfolios including emerging market stocks.

Similar results occurred for the most recent five-year period. As shown in Figure 19, from 1990 to 1995, the efficient frontier for portfolios of U.S. and emerging market equities consisted of portfolios with weights in emerging markets from about 10 percent to 100 percent. Note, however, that the tight return scale on Figure 19 indicates that emerging market stocks provided little return premium over U.S. stocks on an arithmetic-return basis, and recall that the geometric mean returns were reversed.

Table 22. Correlations between Pairs of Emerging Country and Regional Markets Based on All Available U.S.-Dollar-Denominated Returns

	Composite	EMA	Europe	Greece	Hungary	Poland	Portugal	Turkey	Jordan	Africa	Nigeria	South Africa	Zimbabwe	Latin America	Argentina	Brazil	Chile	Colombia	Mexico	Peru	Venezuela	Asia	East Asia	China	Korea	Philippines	Taiwan	South Asia	India	Indonesia	Malaysia	Pakistan	Sri Lanka	Thailand
Composite	1.00	0.38	0.38	0.20	0.34	0.34	0.39	0.29	0.12	0.10	−0.07	0.60	0.14	0.68	0.06	0.06	0.43	0.06	0.06	0.30	−0.10	0.79	0.62	0.35	0.24	0.31	0.82	0.51	0.17	0.43	0.54	0.10	0.31	0.43
EMA		1.00	0.89	0.70	0.15	0.15	0.66	0.66	0.18	0.27	0.08	0.95	0.16	0.21	0.05	0.09	0.14	0.15	0.13	−0.04	−0.02	0.21	0.12	0.30	−0.05	0.06	0.26	0.28	0.13	0.30	0.20	0.03	−0.14	0.27
Europe			1.00	0.76	0.14	0.23	0.75	0.71	0.04	0.10	−0.07	0.37	0.13	0.24	0.05	0.03	0.15	0.16	0.16	−0.09	−0.02	0.23	0.17	0.33	0.00	0.13	0.27	0.26	0.09	0.31	0.23	0.01	−0.01	0.29
Greece				1.00	0.45	0.13	0.44	0.25	0.08	0.15	0.07	0.31	0.12	0.14	0.05	0.00	0.15	0.22	0.04	0.12	0.01	0.07	0.04	0.22	−0.07	0.13	0.09	0.14	0.10	0.19	0.04	−0.05	0.23	0.21
Hungary					1.00	0.34	0.58	−0.05	0.09	0.63	0.55	0.14	0.13	0.57	0.41	0.47	0.47	0.28	0.45	0.32	0.00	0.10	0.12	−0.08	0.35	0.01	0.04	0.06	0.50	0.28	0.04	0.13	0.25	0.02
Poland						1.00	0.46	0.07	0.36	0.18	0.13	0.03	0.36	0.40	0.28	0.27	0.09	0.27	0.40	0.15	0.38	0.23	0.09	0.16	0.22	0.20	0.35	0.34	0.29	0.36	0.32	0.28	0.25	0.14
Portugal							1.00	0.25	−0.06	−0.07	−0.10	0.43	−0.05	0.36	0.00	0.12	0.20	0.15	0.31	0.24	−0.02	0.24	0.31	0.27	0.02	0.14	0.17	0.28	0.10	0.20	0.19	0.03	0.05	0.27
Turkey								1.00	−0.06	0.07	−0.02	0.17	0.00	0.19	0.19	0.08	0.00	0.01	0.15	−0.21	−0.06	0.06	0.20	0.27	0.14	0.14	0.04	0.28	0.10	0.23	0.24	0.02	−0.05	0.21
Jordan									1.00	−0.02	0.06	−0.37	0.00	0.02	0.00	0.08	0.06	−0.03	−0.03	0.41	0.02	0.06	−0.07	−0.02	−0.13	0.09	0.04	0.15	0.14	0.15	0.06	0.14	−0.05	0.08
Africa										1.00	0.75	1.00	0.61	0.09	0.03	0.01	0.13	0.09	0.02	0.30	0.10	−0.02	−0.05	0.10	0.03	0.01	−0.10	0.03	0.07	0.08	−0.07	0.02	0.13	−0.07
Nigeria											1.00	−0.31	0.04	0.04	0.03	0.05	0.07	0.22	−0.05	0.15	0.05	−0.11	−0.08	−0.04	0.08	−0.01	−0.14	−0.12	0.01	0.05	−0.16	0.07	0.03	−0.10
South Africa												1.00	−0.37	0.15	0.19	−0.09	0.21	0.34	0.34	0.17	−0.14	0.62	0.69	0.15	0.48	0.38	0.56	0.46	0.04	0.11	0.51	−0.03	−0.14	0.44
Zimbabwe													1.00	0.13	−0.04	0.04	0.14	−0.01	0.06	0.30	0.21	0.03	−0.05	0.11	−0.07	0.13	−0.02	0.12	0.10	0.22	0.09	0.01	−0.01	−0.01
Latin America														1.00	0.32	0.07	0.51	0.08	0.83	0.52	0.14	0.24	0.19	0.22	0.08	0.12	0.28	0.23	0.12	0.22	0.30	0.08	0.44	0.20
Argentina															1.00	0.01	0.10	−0.07	0.16	0.47	0.05	−0.07	−0.07	0.06	−0.09	−0.03	−0.03	0.00	0.15	−0.06	−0.09	0.00	0.30	−0.01
Brazil																1.00	0.05	0.07	0.00	0.13	−0.03	0.03	0.05	0.33	0.00	0.07	0.06	0.01	0.01	0.12	0.09	−0.01	0.37	−0.05
Chile																	1.00	−0.07	0.16	0.57	−0.13	0.17	0.13	0.17	0.05	0.25	0.26	0.15	0.10	0.25	0.18	0.04	0.22	0.13
Colombia																		1.00	0.16	0.05	0.14	0.03	0.06	−0.37	−0.03	0.13	0.09	0.02	−0.01	0.13	−0.01	0.40	0.36	0.08
Mexico																			1.00	0.47	−0.01	0.28	0.24	0.08	0.13	0.13	0.33	0.23	0.04	0.18	0.35	0.08	0.10	0.24
Peru																				1.00	0.14	0.13	0.04	0.01	0.31	0.19	−0.09	0.19	0.09	0.16	0.04	0.26	0.41	0.32
Venezuela																					1.00	−0.13	−0.17	0.33	−0.08	−0.06	−0.16	0.02	0.04	0.04	0.01	0.08	0.17	−0.04
Asia																						1.00	0.86	0.33	0.47	0.34	0.86	0.60	0.19	0.41	0.56	0.10	0.09	0.50
East Asia																							1.00	0.26	0.69	0.27	0.93	0.20	−0.03	0.28	0.29	0.06	0.39	0.25
China																								1.00	0.06	0.23	0.03	0.31	0.19	0.26	0.29	−0.17	0.02	0.22
Korea																									1.00	0.16	0.07	0.08	0.00	0.02	0.12	0.05	0.37	0.04
Philippines																										1.00	0.19	0.38	−0.04	0.54	0.39	0.14	−0.01	0.37
Taiwan																											1.00	0.26	−0.08	0.29	0.27	0.07	0.17	0.39
South Asia																												1.00	0.54	0.54	0.85	0.16	0.50	0.69
India																													1.00	0.08	0.01	0.03	0.00	0.12
Indonesia																														1.00	0.46	0.11	0.46	0.50
Malaysia																															1.00	0.08	0.00	0.56
Pakistan																																1.00	0.40	0.19
Sri Lanka																																	1.00	0.02
Thailand																																		1.00

Note: Correlations between each pair of countries are for full period for which data are available for both countires.

Figure 17. Risk versus Return for Combinations of Emerging Market Stocks and U.S. Stocks, December 1975–June 1995

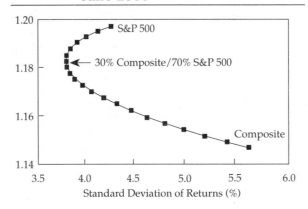

Figure 18. Risk versus Return for Combinations of Emerging Market Stocks and U.S. Stocks, June 1985–June 1995

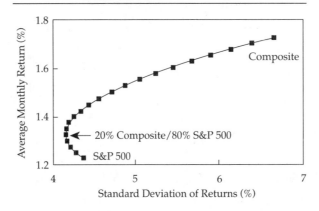

Figure 19. Risk versus Return for Combinations of Emerging Market Stocks and U.S. Stocks, June 1990–June 1995

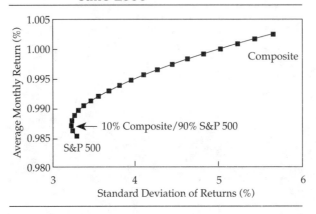

Figures 20–23 present efficient portfolio combinations of U.S. stocks (the S&P 500) and various regional emerging market portfolios. The efficient portfolio combinations of Latin American and U.S. stocks in Figure 22 reveal particularly well the diversification benefits of emerging markets. Although the Latin American markets have been substantially more volatile than the U.S. market, the addition of Latin American stocks to a U.S. stock portfolio over the 1975–95 period could have increased the portfolio's realized rate of return while reducing overall portfolio volatility. For example, the lowest risk portfolio on the efficient frontier consisted of 90 percent S&P 500 and 10 percent Latin American stocks and produced a rate of return in excess of the return experienced by U.S. stocks alone. A similar relationship occurred between U.S. and Asian stocks (Figure 23). In this instance, the efficient portfolio consisted of 70 percent S&P 500 and 30 percent Asian stocks and provided the least risky portfolio on the efficient frontier but still at a rate of return in excess of the S&P 500 alone.

The less mature African and European emerging markets failed to provide meaningful diversification benefits for U.S. investors, largely because stocks in these markets provided low rates of return during the observed time period. For example, Figure 21 shows that the addition of a small portion of higher risk, lower return African stocks to a U.S. stock portfolio would have resulted in a portfolio with less variability than the S&P 500 for the 1975–95 period but only at the expense of a lower rate of return. A similar effect is exhibited in Figure 20 for the emerging European markets.

Figure 20. Risk versus Return: Europe and the S&P 500, December 1975–June 1995

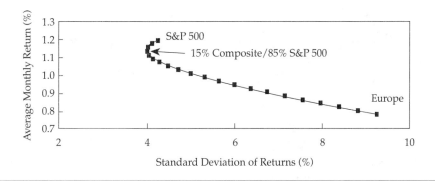

Figure 21. Risk versus Return: Africa and the S&P 500, December 1975–June 1995

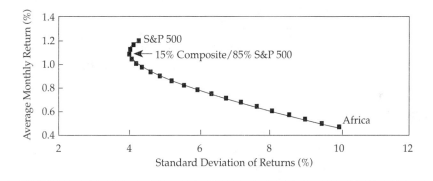

Figure 22. Risk versus Return: Latin America and the S&P 500, December 1975–June 1995

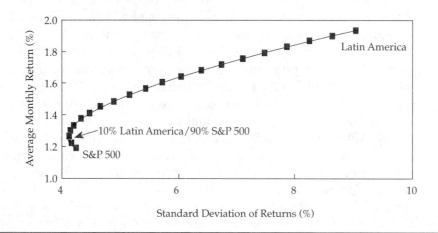

Figure 23. Risk versus Return: Asia and the S&P 500, December 1975– June 1995

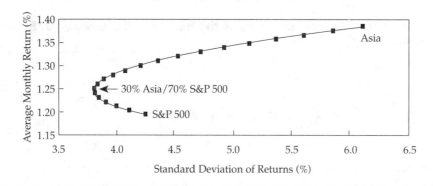

Many U.S. portfolio managers view emerging market investments as a potential component of their international (i.e., non-U.S.) portfolios. Within that international portfolio, the Europe/Australia/Far East (EAFE) Index maintained by Morgan Stanley Capital International (MSCI) is often viewed as the reference portfolio. Figure 24 shows that the diversification benefits of emerging markets have been present for an EAFE-based portfolio as well as for an S&P 500-based portfolio. The minimum-variance combination of EAFE with the Composite included an approximately 40 percent investment in emerging markets when data for the full sample period were used.

Table 21 showed that the correlations between the S&P 500 compound mean rates of return and the compound mean rates of return of individual emerging markets varied widely. Accordingly, configurations of the efficient frontiers representing combinations of the individual emerging markets with the U.S. market vary substantially. For example, as might be expected, the larger, more developed of the individual emerging markets have provided relatively attractive diversification benefits when combined with U.S. stocks. The efficient combinations of stocks from Thailand and the United States depicted in Figure 25 provide a representative example. The inclusion of 20 percent Thai stocks with 80 percent S&P 500 stocks

©The Research Foundation of the ICFA

Figure 24. Risk versus Return: Composite and the EAFE Index, December 1975–June 1995

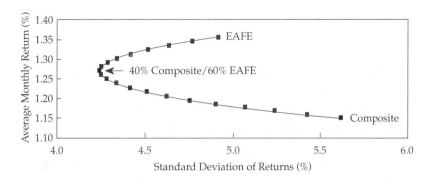

Figure 25. Risk versus Return: Thailand and the S&P 500, December 1975–June 1995

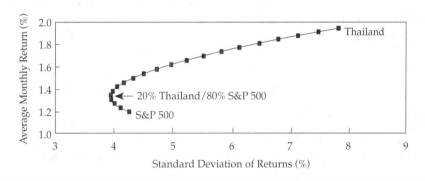

would have produced a meaningfully higher rate of return at substantially lower variability than the S&P 500 alone.

In contrast, many of the small, new emerging markets do not by themselves provide meaningful diversification benefits to stock portfolios based on developed domestic markets. The correlations in some instances are not low enough to offset the effects of very high volatility in the emerging market. For example, Figure 26

Figure 26. Risk versus Return: Poland and the S&P 500, December 1975–June 1995

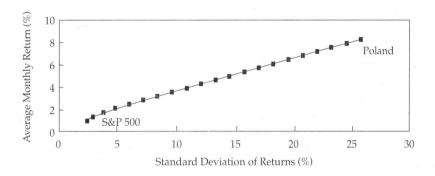

shows that the lowest risk "combination" of U.S. and Polish stocks is composed entirely of U.S. stocks. Thus, only by accepting risk greater than for the S&P 500 would an investor add Polish stocks by themselves to a U.S. portfolio.

Changes in Portfolios across Time

The previous sections showed that emerging markets offer important diversification benefits to the investor holding a portfolio of U.S. equities or of equities related to the EAFE Index. In this section, we examine whether the diversification benefits hold consistently over time. We note the time variation in correlations and examine the construction of portfolios across time, including a graphical analysis of the efficient combinations of U.S. and emerging market portfolios.

Changes in Efficient Combinations of Emerging Markets with the S&P 500. Figure 27 illustrates the change over time that took place in the *ex post* risk–return trade-off between the Composite and the S&P 500 between the roughly two 10-year periods of our data. The first period depicted in Figure 27 is the 9 1/2-year period from the start of the sample, December 1975 through June 1985; the second period is the subsequent 10 years, June 1985 through June 1995. For simplicity, we will refer to these periods as 20- and 10-year periods; the most recent 5-year period is June 1990 through June 1995. The lower graph is for roughly the first 10 years, and the upper graph is for the most recent decade. The two points that represent 100 percent investment in the S&P 500 are nearly in the same location on the graph, but the points representing 100 percent investment in emerging markets are separated by a large distance in risk–return space. In the earlier-period graph, the minimum-variance combination occurs at approximately 50 percent investment in emerging markets, but in the later period, the minimum-variance point is at about a 20 percent investment in emerging markets. Furthermore, emerging markets were dominated in risk–return space in the earlier-period graph but not in the later one.

Consider the minimum-variance point in the earlier period. As mentioned, that point occurs at about a 50 percent investment in emerging markets. Investors who derived that value in the first period might decide that investing 50 percent of their

Figure 27. Risk versus Return: Composite and the S&P 500, December 1975–June 1985 versus June 1985–June 1995

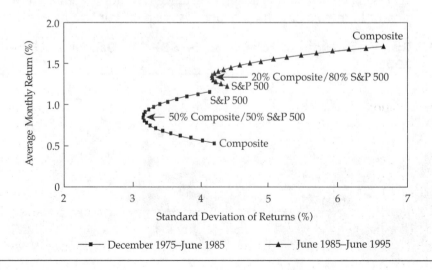

money in emerging markets would sharply reduce the risk of their U.S. portfolios. Where would they be in the later period? Rather than lowering risk relative to the S&P 500, their emerging market investments would have increased risk. Therein lies the problem of using historical data to construct portfolios. As markets change over time, the characteristics of those markets in risk–return terms also change, so what effect the portfolio decisions an investor makes in one period will have on the portfolio returns in the next period is difficult to foretell.

Changes in Correlations between Emerging Markets and the U.S. Market over Time. Table 23 shows selected correlation coefficients between various emerging country markets or regions and the S&P 500. The table illustrates the sometimes sharp changes that have taken place in correlations over time. The table separates selected correlations into those for the June 1985–June 1990 period and those for the June 1990–June 1995 period—the two most recent five-year periods in our study. These changes help explain the difficulty in using risk–return trade-offs for portfolio construction.

Table 23. Illustrative Changes in Correlations between the S&P 500 and Selected Emerging Markets

Market	June 1985–June 1990	June 1990–June 1995
Combinations of markets		
Composite	0.31	0.41
Latin America	0.41	0.38
Asia	0.24	0.32
Markets with increasing correlations		
Argentina	−0.02	0.30
Brazil	−0.03	0.43
Greece	0.07	0.29
Indonesia	−0.15	0.34
Portugal	0.17	0.43
Taiwan	0.08	0.28
Zimbabwe	−0.30	0.03
Markets with decreasing correlations		
Korea	0.31	0.06
India	0.02	−0.16

The first set of results is for correlations of the S&P 500 with the Composite and two regional indexes. The table then shows changes in correlations for seven of the markets that showed increases in correlation with the S&P 500 of at least 0.20 and changes for those markets for which correlations with the S&P 500 decreased. Note that the correlations of the Composite, the Latin America, and the Asia indexes with the S&P 500 changed relatively little between the two periods. Those results are sharply at variance with the story for the individual markets. Apparently, correlation is more stable among broadly diversified portfolios than between individual, narrow markets and a broadly diversified portfolio such as the S&P 500.

Of the markets whose correlations with the S&P 500 increased, the largest change was for Indonesia, whose correlation coefficient rose from −0.15 to a positive 0.34, a change of 0.49. Brazil increased by a slightly smaller amount, from −0.03 to 0.43, a change of 0.46. The tendency of these markets toward increased association with the U.S. market may be a result of the integration of capital markets and expansion of global trade among the nations used in the analysis. For such reasons, apparently excellent diversification vehicles in one period may turn out to be mediocre for the task in a subsequent period.

Only two markets showed decreased correlations with the U.S. market. Korea fell from a relatively high (among emerging markets) 0.31 correlation coefficient in the earlier period to 0.06 in the later period. India fell from a slightly positive value to –0.16.

Changes in Correlations among Emerging Markets over Time. Using the correlation data from Table 22 for the nine markets for which data were available for the full study period (Argentina, Brazil, Chile, Greece, India, Mexico, South Korea, Thailand, and Zimbabwe) and the markets' standard deviations, we constructed efficient sets of emerging market portfolios for the first decade and the second decade. The curved line with the square boxes in Figure 28 represents portfolio combinations for the period of June 1985 to June 1995. Separately, we calculated the efficient frontier from *ex post* data on the nine markets in the 1975–85 period. We identified five points along that earlier frontier that we could use to determine how efficient portfolios from the period would have performed in the 1985–95 period. The five prior-period efficient portfolios are indicated in Figure 28 by the cluster of circles in the lower left area. The prior-period efficient portfolios are not on the efficient frontier in the later period. Thus, identifying efficient portfolios in one period is no assurance that those portfolios will be efficient in a later period.

As an alternative way of demonstrating the instability of portfolios across time, we identified the portfolio weights of the minimum-variance portfolios for the same two periods and same emerging markets used in Figure 28. Table 24 shows those weights. Dramatic shifts occurred between the two periods in the composition of the minimum-variance portfolio. For example, the weight of Greece fell from 24 percent to 8 percent, the weight of Mexico fell from 9 percent to zero, and the weight of Brazil fell from 11 percent to 2 percent. In sharp contrast, Zimbabwe's weight rose from 2 percent to 24 percent and Korea's rose from 9 percent to 25 percent.

Conditional Expectations and Emerging Market Portfolios. Because market performances and correlations between market returns change from one time

Figure 28. Emerging Markets Efficient Frontier, July 1985–June 1995

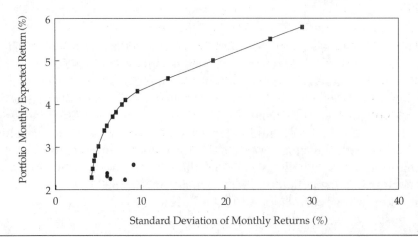

Note: The circles represent *ex post* performance for portfolios based on weights from *ex ante* optimization. The weights making up these inefficient portfolios for this period produced results on the efficient frontier calculated for December 31, 1975, through June 1995.

Table 24. Weights in the Minimum-Variance Portfolios for the Nine Emerging Markets in the EMDB Beginning December 1975

Market	December 1975– June 1985	June 1985– June 1995
Greece	24%	8%
Thailand	22	11
India	21	15
Brazil	11	2
Korea	9	25
Mexico	9	0
Chile	3	13
Zimbabwe	2	24
Argentina	0	2

period to another, investors and managers can find opportunities to improve their portfolio asset allocation decisions. For example, when a portfolio manager selects portfolios based on historical means, variances, and correlations, that process is called "unconditional optimization." The process produces efficient portfolios based on *ex post* data, and after the fact, the manager has no difficulty deciding which asset allocations would have produced efficient portfolios. The procedure is considered "unconditional" because expected returns, variances, and correlations are simply estimated at their previous values without adjustment for the current state of the market. The procedure implies that, because stock returns are not predictable, one's best guess about future performance is the historical average. Basing asset allocation decisions on historical measures, however, without adjusting them to market realities may be misleading.

Instead, on an *ex ante* basis, the optimization procedure should make use of the best available forecasts for returns, variances, and correlations. If stock returns can be partially predicted, asset allocation conditioned on those forecasts will allow managers to make superior asset allocation decisions.

Conditional expectations techniques such as those applied by Harvey (1994) condition the estimates of portfolio parameters on the state of the market. (For example, in the market for U.S. securities, researchers have observed, when dividend yields are low relative to historical norms, subsequent average returns on U.S. stocks tend to be low.) Harvey compared unconditional optimization procedures with procedures that condition expectations on the state of the market as indicated by world and local information variables.[1] He found that both procedures show the diversification benefit of adding emerging markets to portfolios of developed markets but that conditional expectations methods were superior. The unconditional procedures result in improved returns (relative to a zero allocation to emerging markets) for a given level of risk because, even though correlations are changing, the correlations between emerging and developed markets are remaining low. When conditional expectations methods were used, however, the return for a given level of volatility more than doubled.

---

[1]The world variables included the lagged world return, the lagged return on a 10-country currency index, the lagged MSCI world dividend yield, the lagged MSCI earnings-to-price ratio, and the lagged short-term Eurodollar rate of interest. Local information variables consisted of the lagged country equity return in local currency terms, the lagged change in the country's currency exchange rate per U.S. dollar, the lagged country dividend yield, and the lagged country earnings-to-price ratio.

Conclusion

Stocks in emerging markets are generally riskier than their U.S. counterparts. Nevertheless, they can provide important diversification benefits. When properly combined with U.S. stock portfolios, emerging market securities can enhance overall portfolio return while maintaining or even reducing portfolio risk. The reason is that, on average, the returns of emerging stock markets are not highly correlated with each other or with the U.S. stock market.

When dealing with emerging markets, applying inputs estimated in one period to portfolio choices in a subsequent period is dangerous. Chapter 1 demonstrated that fact in terms of arithmetic means, compound means, standard deviations, and compound terminal values. This chapter demonstrated that the identification of efficient or desirable portfolios in one period is no assurance that they will be efficient or desirable in a subsequent period. The analyst or portfolio manager must be cognizant of much more than historical performance and parameter estimates in the selection of alternative markets for portfolios. Moreover, although the low correlations between emerging and developed stock market returns provide diversification opportunities for investors even if only historical data are used, properties of portfolios and their performance in terms of risk and return can be greatly enhanced if investors use forecasted inputs for asset allocation decisions.

©The Research Foundation of the ICFA

3. Investability in Emerging Markets

Even before considering investments in emerging markets, investors should note that indexes based on IFC (International Finance Corporation) data do not include all the securities in a market. For example, a late-1996 *Wall Street Journal* article on India's equity markets pointed out that 7,895 distinct equities were listed in the Indian markets at the time.[1] The IFC's Emerging Markets Data Base (EMDB), however, included data on only 138 Indian equities as of June 1995. Therefore, the real nature of a market may be quite different from the view of it by the EMDB.

Moreover, among the 138 Indian securities contained in the EMDB, the IFC has identified only 101 as *investable* by foreign investors. Because the opportunities available to domestic investors may be different from those available to foreign investors and because performance analysis that ignores the feasibility of investing in certain securities risks misstating the performance actually achievable in the market, the question considered in this chapter is whether the performance results described in Chapters 1 and 2 based on the full EMDB continue to hold when the data are further limited to the set of investable securities.

The IFC established its investability data in December 1988, so only relatively recent data reflect this measure. When we used these data in this study, we included total returns beginning in December 1988 or compound values starting at a value of US$1.00 at the end of November 1988. Because investment performance varies over time, readers should keep in mind the short time period for which investability data exist; a longer time period would increase the confidence readers could have in the results. These data are for the most recent periods of the study, however, and thus particularly pertinent to present circumstances in the markets.

The Investable Universe

Foreigners are prohibited altogether from investing in the equities of some markets. In other markets, the fraction of a given company's stock that may be held by foreigners is restricted. In South Korea, for example, the restriction is typically 10 percent of outstanding shares. In Thailand, foreign limits exist, but when the limits are reached, shares held by foreigners may trade on the Alien Board. In some markets, foreign investors are limited to holding only certain classes of equity; for example, China provides A Shares for domestic investors while limiting foreign investors to B Shares. Foreign ownership may be restricted by the government of a country or the articles of incorporation of a specific company.

The IFC Investable Index includes the stocks of 25 of the 26 countries covered in the EMDB; Nigeria is considered to be not investable. The IFC identifies a security as investable under certain conditions.[2] One condition is that foreigners not be

---

[1]Sumit Sharma, "Many Investors in Indian Stocks Have Nothing but Woe to Share," *Wall Street Journal* (November 25, 1996):C1.

[2]The IFC's publication titled "IFC Index Methodology" describes the investable indexes and the various restrictions placed on foreign ownership.

restricted from buying the security. Under the IFC's definition, securities are not investable if foreigners are prohibited from holding them. For each security in which foreign holding is allowed but limited, the EMDB identifies the fraction of that security that can be held by foreigners. The remaining conditions are not explicitly stated by the IFC. Presumably, the size, liquidity, and industry factors initially used for inclusion of securities in the EMDB are applied more strictly in identifying investable securities.

For this study, we began with the IFC's designation of securities investable by foreign investors and constructed our own indexes based on the IFC's definition. When we refer to an investable index here, we mean we have used the IFC's identification of investable securities, not that we are using the IFC's Investable Index.

So that the results reported here can be compared with results reported earlier in the monograph, comparisons in this chapter are made between the investable securities (Investables) and all the securities (All) in a market or region included in the EMDB, rather than between "investables" and "uninvestables." Investables is a subset of All.

One final note: We do not report separate results for Thailand in the comparison of investable securities with the EMDB set of securities because Thailand's system of foreign trading, the Alien Board system, can lead to distinct price differences between shares traded among foreigners and those traded among Thai citizens. The EMDB does not separately identify the prices when the same security trades at different prices on and off the Alien Board. Thus, performance of truly investable securities cannot be distinguished from performance of uninvestable securities in Thailand.

Performance Comparisons: Investables versus All

The performance comparisons in this section are of value-weighted portfolios of Investables with value-weighted portfolios constructed from All securities. Figure 29 compares the compound value of a US$1.00 investment in Investables with the same investment in All over the period from late 1988 through mid-1995.[3] As the figure demonstrates, Investables have consistently outperformed All since September 1989. A foreign investor has indeed had access to performance in emerging markets comparable to that available to domestic investors on an overall basis.

Table 25 breaks down the aggregate results to a broad set of regional indexes to contrast Investables with All on a regional basis. The table shows the compound value of US$1.00 invested for the period covered in each of eight regional indexes, including the investable subset from our Emerging Markets Composite Value-Weighted Index (the Composite). The compound value of an investment of US$1.00 in Investables is greater than a comparable investment in All in every case except those of Europe and the Europe/Mideast/Africa (EMA) index. Note that monthly geometric mean returns compare in the same manner because the higher a compound return value, the higher the geometric mean.

An important issue for the investor to consider is why Investables perform better than All. A likely explanation is that the opening up of emerging markets and the lessening of restrictions led to substantial flows of portfolio capital into the markets that opened. That capital could only flow into securities for which foreign investment was not prohibited. The demand for investable securities thus rose sharply and, accordingly, so did the prices. Although this explanation may appear reasonable,

---

[3]Some markets were added to the database later than others and do not have data available for the full period covered in this chapter, December 1988 through June 1995. See Table 1 for dates when markets were added to the EMDB.

Figure 29. Performance of Investables versus Performance of All, data from end November 1988–June 1995

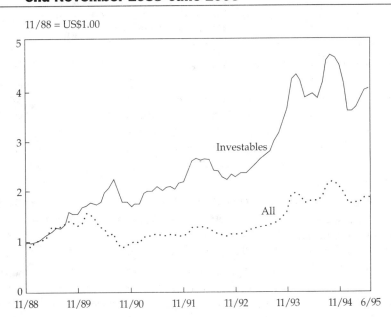

Table 25. Relative Performance of Investables, December 1988–June 1995

Market	Compound Index Value of US$1.00 Invested		Monthly Geometric Mean Return		Standard Deviation	
	All	Investables	All	Investables	All	Investables
Composite	1.840	3.988	0.775%	1.766%	6.110%	5.715%
EMA	2.759	2.674	1.293	1.253	8.497	10.220
Europe	2.173	2.029	0.987	0.899	10.109	10.995
Africa[a]	2.765	2.845	4.329	4.453	10.704	9.445
Latin America	6.197	7.720	2.336	2.621	7.456	13.094
Asia	1.409	3.146	0.435	1.461	7.146	6.613
East Asia	1.003	1.740	0.004	0.703	8.899	9.153
South Asia	3.027	3.428	1.412	1.572	5.991	6.867

[a]Values for Africa are calculated from June 1993 through June 1995. Nigerian securities were not identified as investable by the IFC.

rigorous tests of the explanation have not been conducted. The cause of the difference remains open for further study.

The last two columns of Table 25 allow comparison of standard deviations of returns for the Investables and All. The results are mixed. For the Composite, Asia, and Africa, standard deviation is lower for the Investables than for All. The opposite holds for Latin America, South Asia, East Asia, the EMA, and Europe. The reason is not clear. The effects of foreign investors might be expected to increase the volatility of foreign-owned securities. Also, because All contains securities not available in Investables, All may generally be more diverse and have lower risk. Counteracting those influences, to the extent that the Investables group tends to be biased toward larger and more liquid securities, Investables may tend to be less volatile.

Portfolio Characteristics of Investables

In Chapter 2, we examined the results of combining emerging markets and the S&P 500 Index in portfolios. In this section, we compare the performance of portfolios containing Investables plus the S&P 500 with the performance of portfolios containing All plus the S&P 500.

The results for the Composite Investables or All securities combined with the S&P 500 are shown in Figure 30. The results come from applying standard Markowitz portfolio analysis to the following data: The mean monthly rate of return and monthly standard deviation of return for the S&P 500 for the study period were, respectively, 1.18 percent and 3.50 percent; the Composite Investables for the period had an arithmetic average monthly return of 1.93 percent and standard deviation of 5.72 percent; for All, the corresponding values were 0.96 percent and 6.11 percent.

Figure 30. Portfolios of Investables and the S&P 500 versus Portfolios of All and the S&P 500: Combinations Based on Monthly Returns, December 1988–June 1995

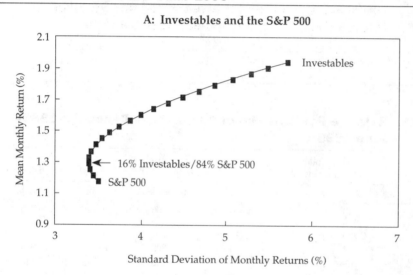

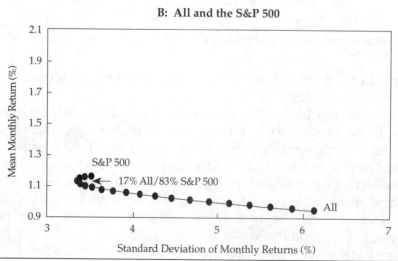

Note: Minimum-variance portfolios are, respectively, 15.9 percent Investable/84.1 percent S&P 500 and 17.1 percent All/82.9 percent S&P 500.

Correlation coefficients of these emerging markets with the S&P 500 were 0.3750 for the Investables and 0.2691 for All.

The Investables produced a superior *ex post* set of portfolio combinations with the S&P 500 when compared with All. Although the sets of emerging market securities produced minimum-variance combinations with the S&P 500 with similar weights, the All portfolio was dominated (in mean–variance terms) by the S&P 500. Certain combinations of the Investables portfolio with the S&P 500, however, dominated the S&P 500: Using Investables as the emerging market vehicle produced a set of portfolio combinations with lower standard deviations and higher compound mean returns than the S&P 500 by itself. The investment opportunity set was dramatically more efficient with investable securities than with the full set of emerging market securities.

Tables 26 and 27 develop the results shown in Figure 30. Table 26 shows the correlations between each regional or country market and the S&P 500 and standard deviations of monthly returns over the period for which data were available in each

Table 26. Correlations of Emerging Markets with the S&P 500 and Standard Deviations for Investables and All Emerging Market Securities, December 1988–June 1995

	Correlation with S&P 500		Standard Deviation	
Market	All	Investables	All	Investables
Composite	0.2691	0.3750	6.11%	5.72%
EMA	0.0109	–0.0184	8.50	10.22
Europe	0.0019	–0.0135	10.11	10.99
Greece	0.0450	0.0466	12.51	13.53
Hungary	0.3505	0.3344	14.67	15.56
Jordan	0.1952	0.1862	5.28	5.69
Poland	0.2785	0.2805	25.70	25.68
Portugal	0.3168	0.2969	6.93	7.26
Turkey	–0.1415	–0.1479	20.49	20.88
South Africa[a]	0.2826	0.2869	7.34	7.42
Zimbabwe[b]	0.0390	–0.1085	11.08	11.70
Latin America	0.2908	0.1131	7.46	13.09
Argentina	0.0687	0.0703	29.81	30.09
Brazil	0.4267	0.4600	16.27	16.95
Chile	0.2184	0.2182	7.59	7.67
Colombia	0.0215	0.0806	11.81	11.74
Mexico	0.2652	0.3121	10.09	10.63
Peru	0.1204	0.1332	13.74	14.58
Venezuela	–0.0458	–0.0980	14.45	19.38
Asia	0.2120	0.4371	7.15	6.61
East Asia	0.1620	0.3758	8.90	9.15
China	0.0610	0.3042	23.99	12.89
Korea	–0.0487	–0.0557	7.82	7.65
Philippines	0.3535	0.3782	9.78	10.84
Taiwan	0.0513	0.0505	11.60	11.63
South Asia	0.2998	0.4263	5.99	6.87
India	0.0911	0.0912	8.13	8.24
Indonesia	0.3401	0.3438	8.82	9.20
Malaysia	0.3911	0.3780	7.15	7.49
Pakistan	0.0387	0.0479	10.17	11.41
Sri Lanka	–0.1231	–0.1158	9.83	10.46

[a]Data for South Africa start January 1994.
[b]Data for Zimbabwe start June 1993.

Table 27. Portfolio Minimum-Variance Weights of Emerging Markets Combined with the S&P 500, December 1988–June 1995

	All	Investables
Composite	17.07%	15.89%
EMA	14.24	10.94
Europe	10.66	9.52
Greece	6.24	5.27
Hungary	0.00	0.00
Jordon	26.23	22.98
Poland	0.00	0.00
Portugal	10.16	9.43
Turkey	4.95	4.91
South Africa	9.68	9.15
Zimbabwe	8.14	10.57
Latin America	8.869	4.08
Argentina	0.57	0.54
Brazil	0.00	0.00
Chile	11.10	10.78
Colombia	7.59	6.23
Mexico	3.04	0.63
Peru	3.42	2.58
Venezuela	6.46	4.71
Asia	13.19	5.99
East Asia	8.86	0.30
China	1.24	0.00
Korea	17.87	18.65
Philippines	0.18	0.00
Taiwan	7.13	7.11
South Asia	16.78	5.16
India	13.20	12.85
Indonesia	2.55	1.58
Malaysia	5.66	4.82
Pakistan	9.63	7.46
Sri Lanka	14.04	12.68

Note: The S&P 500 total returns index had a standard deviation of monthly returns of 3.50 percent during the sample period.

market. In both cases, data are shown for Investables and All. Note in the correlation values that 13 of the 31 reported values are lower for Investables than for All and, in general, the correlations for Investables are very similar to those for All. The standard deviations form more distinctive patterns: Only five of the standard deviations are smaller for Investables than for All, perhaps a reflection of the greater diversification available when more securities are included in an opportunity set.

One of the most important results of Chapter 2 is the finding that some combinations of emerging markets with developed markets lie on the efficient frontier. That result is important because it means that combining emerging market securities with U.S. investments can reduce portfolio risk even though the emerging markets are themselves riskier than the S&P 500. Table 27 examines whether that result holds in the case of the Investables. Minimum-variance weights for each of the markets or regions are shown for portfolios consisting of the corresponding market and the S&P 500 using either the Investables set or the All set. The weights were calculated under the assumption of no short sales (that is, their minimum value was restricted to zero).[4] In the case of All, the minimum-variance combination has no positive investment in emerging markets in only three combinations—the S&P 500 with Brazil, Hungary, and Poland. When only Investables are used, there are five cases of zero investment in the emerging market in combination with the S&P 500 (three of which are the same as for combinations with All): *Brazil*, China, the Philippines, *Hungary*, and *Poland*. Note also that, on average, the investments in emerging markets are slightly less in the case of Investables than in the case of All but the results are very similar in the two sets. In two cases, South Korea and Zimbabwe, the minimum-variance combination actually includes more of the emerging market when Investables are used than when All is used, although the differences are not large.

Conclusion

This chapter showed that the results of Chapters 1 and 2 hold to a strong degree when investability is incorporated in performance analysis. The investable subset of EMDB securities actually outperformed the broader set on a compound-returns basis in recent years. The diversification benefits that appear to be available on examining emerging markets continue to be present, for the most part, when practical account is taken of the investability of the securities included in a portfolio.

This chapter did not deal with a number of other practical issues, one of which is information cost. In an era when small investors in the United States have easy access to massive quantities of historical data and financial reports on U.S. securities, the information costs of including emerging market securities are likely to be an impediment to the use of emerging markets in combination with U.S. securities. Other issues are liquidity costs, in the form of bid–ask spreads that are higher than in developed markets; tax laws, which vary widely among emerging markets; and restrictions on the repatriation of funds, which can impede investment in some markets.

---

[4]The minimum-variance weight was calculated from the two-security Markowitz portfolio model: The minimum-variance value is the larger of zero and w^*, where w^* is $(V_{SP500} - C_{EM,SP500})/(V_{EM} + V_{SP500} - 2 \times C_{EM,SP500})$. The terms V_{EM} and V_{SP500} refer, respectively, to the (sample) variances of monthly returns of the corresponding emerging market and the S&P 500, and $C_{EM,SP500}$ is the covariance between the emerging market and the S&P 500. Covariance between the two markets is calculated as correlation between them multiplied by the product of the two markets' standard deviations.

4. Investing in Emerging Markets via Closed-End Funds

Investors who are not inhabitants of the relevant country but want to invest directly in an individual emerging market will be confronted with risks not associated with investments in their domestic markets or in developed nondomestic markets. Some of those risks are very practical ones that are not related to ordinary fluctuations in security values over time. They include the risk that the investor does not understand the laws in the target market that affect the investor's ability to hold a position or repatriate funds. The investor may also incur the risk of misinterpreting accounting information that is presented under a unique set of accounting rules in the market. Even such practical issues as custody and clearing operations may present an unexpected risk to the investor. Given these risks, and the costs of gathering the information required to overcome them, the investor may prefer to buy shares of professionally managed funds that invest in the chosen markets. In this way, the investor can rely on the expertise of professional investment managers who specialize in these markets and spread the costs over a larger investment size.

Two primary types of funds are available through which to invest in emerging markets: open-end (mutual) funds and closed-end funds. A mutual fund has a variable number of shares outstanding; investors can purchase or redeem shares at the fund's net asset value (NAV), which is defined as follows:

$$\text{NAV} = \frac{\text{Market value of securities owned} - \text{Total liabilities}}{\text{Shares outstanding}}.$$

Hence, the number of mutual fund shares outstanding changes as investors purchase and redeem shares. All mutual fund transactions occur at the NAV.

In contrast, closed-end funds have a fixed number of shares outstanding. Closed-end fund shares trade in the open market at a price determined by willing buyers and sellers. Thus, the shares of a closed-end fund may trade at prices different from the fund's underlying NAV.

Although several open-end emerging market funds exist, the majority of the funds investing in these markets are of the closed-end variety. Rarely will a fund investing in the securities of a single country be open ended, largely because of the potential problem of having to sell shares of relatively illiquid securities from the fund's portfolio on short notice in order to accommodate investor redemptions.

Table 28 lists 20 closed-end funds that invest exclusively in emerging markets. Sixteen of the funds, known as "country funds," invest only in the securities of a particular emerging country.[1] The Mexico Fund, which went public on June 11, 1981, is the senior country fund; it is followed by the Korea Fund, which began public trading on August 19, 1984. As of December 31, 1995, these two funds were also the largest

---

[1]More than one country fund exists for several of the individual emerging markets. In those instances, Table 28 lists only the oldest country fund from a particular market.

Table 28. Closed-End Funds of the Emerging Markets

Fund	Date of Inception	Discount or Premium[a]	1995 Expense Ratio	Annual Return since Inception NAV	Market
Argentina	10/11/91	2.7%	1.98%	4.76%	4.16%
Brazil	04/08/88	2.0	1.62	15.37	13.34
Chile	09/27/89	−12.6	1.39	30.43	27.47
China	07/10/92	2.7	2.55	1.77	1.97
First Philippine	11/15/89	−18.4	1.82	15.24	10.54
India Growth	08/19/88	9.9	1.94	8.81	10.38
Indonesia	03/09/90	21.4	1.96	−4.35	−3.46
Korea	08/29/84	4.2	1.32	20.35[b]	17.97[b]
Malaysia	05/04/87	−6.7	1.44	12.86	11.05
Mexico	06/11/81	2.6	1.14	25.06[b]	28.81[b]
New South Africa	03/04/94	−20.7	2.10	21.74	6.08
Pakistan Investment	12/17/93	−19.4	2.20	−27.02	−31.72
Portugal	11/01/89	−12.0	1.41	0.95	−2.16
Taiwan	12/05/86	4.8	2.43	20.22	20.22
Thailand	02/16/88	−11.7	1.30	21.55	19.70
Turkish Investment	12/05/89	8.7	2.16	−8.75	−8.69
Asia Tigers	11/19/93	−11.5	1.65	−0.93	−5.43
Latin American Investment	07/25/90	−7.8	1.72	23.83	21.15
Morgan Stanley Emerging	10/25/91	0.6	1.86	17.18	16.34
Templeton Emerging	02/26/87	13.7	1.73	20.53	21.79

Note: All of these funds trade on the New York Stock Exchange.

[a]Average for 1995.

[b]Last 10 years only.

Source: Morningstar Closed-End Funds.

funds; the Mexico Fund had net assets of US$750 million, and the Korea Fund had net assets amounting to US$747 million. The remaining 14 country funds went public from 1986 to 1994 and range in net assets from US$32 million (Turkish Investment Fund) to US$336 million (Brazil Fund). As of June 30, 1995, 10 markets in the EMDB were not represented by a U.S.-based closed-end country fund—Colombia, Greece, Hungary, Jordan, Nigeria, Peru, Poland, Sri Lanka, Venezuela, and Zimbabwe.

In addition to the country funds, two funds (Asia Tigers and Latin American Investment) invest in the securities of emerging markets in particular regions; two other funds listed in Table 28 (Morgan Stanley and Templeton) invest in diversified portfolios containing securities from many emerging markets. The Templeton Emerging Markets Fund, having gone public on February 27, 1987, is the oldest broadly diversified emerging market fund and also, with net assets of US$242 million as of December 31, 1995, the largest.

Historical Performance of Closed-End Emerging Market Funds

An investor contemplating participating in a closed-end fund needs to understand how effectively the fund shares represent the performance of the underlying securities of the relevant market(s). Most emerging market closed-end funds trade on the New York Stock Exchange (NYSE), which has caused some investors to question whether the prices of fund shares are influenced by movements in the U.S. stock market. These investors also contend that a change in a fund's discount from or premium to NAV may cause the fund's performance to differ from the performance of its portfolio of securities. Finally, these investors express concern about the abilities of the funds' managers to generate returns at least as high as those of the underlying markets.

Table 29 allows comparison of the emerging market funds' performance relative to their underlying market(s). The table presents rates of return and risk information for roughly a five-year period ended June 30, 1995.[2] Also presented are correlations of each individual fund and its market with the S&P 500 Index.

Over the period studied, the average monthly geometric mean rate of return for the 16 country funds was 0.35 percent, as compared with a 0.70 percent monthly return for the relevant country indexes. For all 20 funds, the average monthly return was 0.45 percent, versus a 0.79 percent return for the relevant markets. The monthly geometric mean rate of return for only five country funds (the China Fund, the Indonesia Fund, Mexico Fund, First Philippines Fund, and Taiwan Fund) exceeded the rate of return for their market indexes. The remaining country funds experienced a lower compound mean rate of return than its market index.

One of the causes of the relative underperformance of the country funds is their high expense ratios. *Morningstar Closed-End Funds* reports that the average annual expense ratio for these 16 funds for 1995 was 1.80 percent; the range was from 1.14 percent (the Mexico Fund) to 2.55 percent (the China Fund).

Excluding the two funds with less than a 1½-year history as of June 30, 1995 (the China Fund and the New South Africa Fund), only five country funds recorded a lower standard deviation of returns than their market indexes. Each of the other nine funds experienced greater volatility than its market index. The average monthly standard deviation for the 14 country funds (excluding the two new funds) was 10.91 percent, more than three times the S&P 500's monthly standard deviation of 3.30 percent over the same period. Seven country funds experienced lower compound rates of return and higher volatility than their market benchmarks. The China Fund with only a 2½-year history and the Taiwan Fund with only six months of history were the only country funds to show a higher monthly compound rate of return at lower volatility than its benchmark index.

Both of the broadly diversified emerging market closed-end funds, Morgan Stanley's and Templeton's, provided monthly compound rates of return in excess of their benchmark indexes, the Emerging Markets Composite Index, even though the funds had high expense ratios (for 1995, 1.86 percent for Morgan Stanley and 1.73 percent for Templeton). The two funds also recorded average monthly mean rates of return that were higher than their corresponding index—for Morgan Stanley, 1.58 percent versus 1.25 percent for the index over the same period; for Templeton, 2.24 percent versus 1.00 percent. And the average monthly standard deviation of returns for these funds (7.80 percent for Morgan Stanley and 9.69 percent for Templeton) was lower than the average standard deviation for the individual country funds, which was 10.88 percent but higher than that of the emerging market composite, which was less than 6 percent. On a risk-adjusted basis, the results are mixed for these two diversified funds. The Morgan Stanley Fund underperformed the composite index. The Sharpe Index values were 16.06 percent and 18.02 percent, respectively. The Templeton Fund, which covers 16 more months, achieved a higher risk-adjusted return than the composite (19.03 percent versus 10.76 percent). Apparently the greater diversification among these funds reduced risk, at least relative to the country funds.

Diversification Benefits of Closed-End Funds

In order to provide meaningful diversification benefits to U.S. investors when

---

[2]For any fund with less than a five-year history, rates of return and standard deviations were computed from the first full quarter of the fund's existence through June 30, 1995.

Table 29. Rates of Return and Standard Deviations for Closed-End Funds and Value-Weighted Market Portfolios plus Correlations with the S&P 500, Various Time Periods

Fund or Market	Average Monthly Return	Standard Deviation	Geometric Mean Return	Compounded Value of US$1.00	Correlation with S&P 500	Period Covered
S&P 500	0.99%	3.30%	0.93%	1.7451	1.0000	6/90–6/95
Argentina Fund	0.00	9.05	−0.40	0.8370	0.3161	10/91–6/95
Argentina	1.76	12.24	1.04	1.5746	0.1159	10/91–6/95
Brazil Fund	2.55	12.78	1.77	2.8659	0.4704	6/90–6/95
Brazil	3.12	16.52	1.87	3.0447	0.4303	6/90–6/95
Chile Fund	2.93	11.86	2.27	3.8490	0.5011	6/90–6/95
Chile	3.41	8.05	3.10	6.2452	0.3584	6/90–6/95
China Fund	1.36	14.61	0.47	1.1510	0.3095	12/92–6/95
China	0.47	23.99	−1.67	0.6025	0.0610	12/92–6/95
India Growth Fund	1.47	11.59	0.83	1.6444	0.2058	6/90–6/95
India	1.59	10.96	1.03	1.8454	−0.1596	6/90–6/95
Indonesia Fund	0.18	10.97	−0.36	0.8071	0.3745	6/90–6/95
Indonesia	−0.13	8.69	−0.50	0.7402	0.3397	6/90–6/95
Korea Fund	0.79	11.16	0.20	1.1260	0.1506	6/90–6/95
Korea	0.64	7.87	0.35	1.2356	0.0629	6/90–6/95
Malaysia Fund	1.40	9.98	0.93	1.7471	0.4052	6/90–6/95
Malaysia	1.65	7.52	1.37	2.2646	0.3315	6/90–6/95
Mexico Fund	1.87	12.98	1.05	1.8672	0.3499	6/90–6/95
Mexico	1.50	10.82	0.87	1.6865	0.2406	6/90–6/95
New South Africa Fund	1.86	6.81	1.64	1.2765	0.0632	3/94–6/95
South Africa	3.15	7.51	2.88	1.5321	0.1488	3/94–6/95
Pakistan Investment Fund	−4.35	5.50	−4.50	0.4368	0.2093	12/93–6/95
Pakistan	−1.31	5.79	−1.47	0.7661	−0.3163	12/93–6/95
First Philippines Fund	2.22	11.08	1.64	2.6611	0.3297	6/90–6/95
Philippines	2.03	10.02	1.55	2.5143	0.3760	6/90–6/95
Portugal Fund	0.56	10.03	0.07	1.0455	0.5369	6/90–6/95
Portugal	0.33	6.43	0.12	1.0774	0.4297	6/90–6/95
Taiwan Fund	1.03	12.53	0.28	1.1846	0.2983	6/90–6/95
Taiwan	1.05	13.17	0.25	1.1589	0.2774	6/90–6/95
Thailand Fund	1.34	10.45	0.81	1.6261	0.4655	6/90–6/95
Thailand	1.83	9.85	1.37	2.2569	0.3141	6/90–6/95
Turkish Fund	−0.29	12.77	−1.07	0.5246	0.2701	6/90–6/95
Turkey	0.52	17.88	−0.99	0.5500	−0.1186	6/90–6/95
Asia Tigers Fund Inc.	−0.91	11.25	−1.49	0.7514	0.6709	11/93–6/95
Asia	1.00	7.24	0.77	1.1562	0.3529	11/93–6/95
East Asia	1.49	7.95	1.21	1.2565	0.2221	11/93–6/95
South Asia	0.59	7.62	0.32	1.0636	0.4364	11/93–6/95
Latin American Investment Fund	2.55	12.15	1.82	2.8925	0.4972	7/90–6/95
Latin America	2.17	7.52	1.89	3.0207	0.3869	7/90–6/95
Morgan Stanley Emerging Markets Fund	1.58	7.80	1.29	1.7544	0.3688	10/91–6/95
Emerging Market Composite	1.25	5.09	1.13	1.6365	0.2070	10/91–6/95
Templeton Emerging Markets Fund	2.24	9.69	1.78	2.8861	0.6268	6/90–6/95
Emerging Market Composite	1.00	5.66	0.84	1.6567	0.4081	6/90–6/95

combined with domestic stocks, emerging market funds must provide returns that are not highly correlated with the returns of U.S. stocks. Table 29 shows that over the roughly five-year period ended June 30, 1995, the returns of these funds were not highly correlated with S&P 500 returns. Correlation coefficients range from a low of

0.06 (New South Africa Fund) to a high of 0.67 (Asia Tigers Fund).[3] The average correlation coefficient of the 20 funds with the S&P 500 is 0.36. Consequently, emerging market closed-end funds appear to provide diversification benefits to investors holding U.S. stocks.

In addition to correlation, another key consideration with respect to the diversification benefits of an emerging market closed-end fund is the extent to which the fund returns reflect primarily the underlying market rather than outside factors. As noted, some investors have been concerned that the returns of these funds may be considerably affected by movements in the stock markets in which the shares are sold, which would cause the funds to be less-than-perfect proxies for their respective emerging markets. The empirical results provide support for this argument.

As shown in Table 29, for the period studied, the returns of 18 of the 20 closed-end funds were more highly correlated with the S&P 500 than were the returns for their respective benchmark markets. Only the newest fund, the New South Africa Fund, with a brief 15-month performance history, and the First Philippine Fund were less correlated with the S&P 500 than were their underlying market indexes. The average correlation coefficient of the markets is 0.2123, only slightly more than half the magnitude of the average correlation coefficient for the 20 closed-end funds. Therefore, over the observed period, emerging market closed-end funds did not provide as substantial diversification benefits as would have direct (indexed) investments in the underlying securities of the relevant emerging markets.

Conclusion

The availability of closed-end funds that invest in the stocks of emerging markets provides investors with a convenient way to invest in these markets. Because many of these funds trade actively on the NYSE, their shares can be purchased readily at low transaction costs.

A key question is whether these specialized funds can generate rates of return comparable to those of the underlying markets the funds represent and at comparable risk. The relative newness of the funds, and thus the paucity of empirical findings about long-term returns, prevents a definitive answer to this question. Empirical results for the roughly five years ended June 30, 1995, indicate, however, that emerging market closed-end funds provide some diversification benefits to holders of U.S. stock portfolios (as a result of their low correlations with U.S. stocks) but the funds have not been highly representative of their underlying markets. With the exception of the two broadly diversified funds, the funds have, on average, underperformed their respective benchmarks and experienced greater volatility. Of additional importance is the fact that these funds have not provided as meaningful diversification benefits as direct investments in the securities of the underlying markets would have provided because the funds' returns are substantially more correlated with U.S. stocks. If these funds are to provide returns representative of their underlying markets in the future, they must show higher correlations with their market indexes than in the past.

---

[3]If the New South Africa Fund, with only a 1¼-year trading history, is excluded, then the Korea Fund had the lowest correlation with the S&P 500 (0.1506).

Appendix: Monthly Value-Weighted Stock Returns

This appendix reports the monthly returns calculated from International Finance Corporation (IFC) data for the Emerging Markets Composite Value-Weighted Index (the Composite), the subindexes for the Europe/Middle East/Africa (EMA), Europe, Africa, Latin America, Asia, East Asia, and South Asia regions, and the individual country markets. Stock price data begin December 1975; hence, return data begin January 1, 1976, and end June 30, 1995. Table A.1 contains comparable data for the S&P 500 Index and the Morgan Stanley Capital International EAFE (Europe/Australia/Far East) Index.

Table A.1. Composite and Regions in Emerging Markets: Total Value-Weighted Stock Returns, January 1976–June 1995

	S&P 500	EAFE	Composite	EMA	Europe	Africa	Latin America	Asia	East Asia	South Asia
Jan 76	0.1199	0.05	0.0739	0.0623	0.0603	0.0779	−0.0185	0.1683	0.2687	0.1247
Feb 76	−0.0058	−0.01	−0.0039	−0.0247	−0.0159	−0.0924	0.0219	−0.0039	0.0047	−0.0078
Mar 76	0.0326	−0.02	0.0133	−0.0402	−0.0417	−0.0281	0.0845	0.0027	0.0611	−0.0253
Apr 76	−0.0099	−0.01	0.0167	0.0127	0.0149	−0.0054	0.0361	−0.0053	−0.0008	−0.0076
May 76	−0.0073	−0.03	−0.0485	−0.0661	−0.0619	−0.0998	−0.0329	−0.0448	−0.0385	−0.0483
Jun 76	0.0427	0.02	0.0456	0.0341	0.0268	0.0921	0.0465	0.0614	0.0580	0.0633
Jul 76	−0.0068	−0.01	0.0170	−0.0177	−0.0160	−0.0299	0.0410	0.0316	−0.0024	0.0508
Aug 76	0.0014	0.00	0.0008	0.0034	0.0147	−0.0842	−0.0149	0.0203	−0.0376	0.0517
Sep 76	0.0247	−0.02	−0.0771	−0.0067	−0.0330	0.2282	−0.2196	0.0282	0.0131	0.0367
Oct 76	−0.0206	−0.06	−0.0704	−0.0140	−0.0010	−0.1052	−0.2129	0.0067	0.0743	−0.0298
Nov 76	−0.0009	0.01	0.0261	0.0117	0.0226	−0.0594	0.0817	−0.0005	0.0337	−0.0210
Dec 76	0.0540	0.11	0.0666	−0.0004	0.0076	−0.0576	0.1565	0.0729	0.1216	0.0408
Jan 77	−0.0489	−0.01	−0.0279	−0.0390	−0.0287	−0.1180	−0.0974	0.0528	0.1051	0.0155
Feb 77	−0.0151	0.02	0.0147	−0.0120	0.0003	−0.1162	0.0282	0.0322	0.0477	0.0210
Mar 77	−0.0119	0.00	0.0855	0.1079	0.1093	0.0935	0.1168	0.0345	−0.0005	0.0605
Apr 77	0.0014	0.03	0.0541	0.1013	0.1160	−0.0412	0.0650	−0.0105	−0.0539	0.0198
May 77	−0.0150	0.00	0.0175	−0.0504	−0.0533	−0.0168	0.0849	0.0335	0.0478	0.0240
Jun 77	0.0475	0.02	0.0562	0.0867	0.0891	0.0606	0.0568	0.0205	0.0424	0.0055
Jul 77	−0.0151	−0.02	0.0449	0.0257	0.0328	−0.0536	0.0951	0.0121	−0.0122	0.0299
Aug 77	−0.0133	0.04	0.0304	0.0766	0.0837	−0.0109	−0.0714	0.0966	0.0629	0.1208
Sep 77	0.0000	0.03	0.0197	−0.0275	−0.0281	−0.0193	0.0270	0.0688	0.2008	−0.0210
Oct 77	−0.0415	0.03	0.0149	−0.0805	−0.0845	−0.0261	0.0346	0.0994	0.0804	0.1155
Nov 77	0.0370	−0.01	0.0150	0.0327	0.0296	0.0733	0.0686	−0.0490	−0.0259	−0.0684
Dec 77	0.0048	0.04	0.0824	0.0742	0.0657	0.1794	0.0861	0.0868	0.1107	0.0658
Jan 78	−0.0596	0.01	0.0723	0.0146	0.0179	−0.0222	0.1080	0.0935	0.1246	0.0649
Feb 78	−0.0161	0.01	0.0964	−0.0057	−0.0079	−0.0397	0.2795	0.0247	0.0489	0.0027
Mar 78	0.0276	0.07	−0.0047	−0.0103	−0.0096	−0.0562	−0.0105	0.0076	0.0013	0.0135
Apr 78	0.0870	−0.01	0.0498	0.0203	−0.0078	−0.0880	0.1023	0.0161	0.0426	−0.0086
May 78	0.0136	0.02	0.0217	0.0101	0.0051	−0.0374	0.0157	0.0405	0.0544	0.0263
Jun 78	−0.0152	0.05	0.0198	0.0053	0.0097	−0.0165	0.0182	0.0348	0.0516	0.0166
Jul 78	0.0560	0.09	0.0118	0.0094	0.0008	0.1842	−0.0019	0.0303	0.0513	0.0064
Aug 78	0.0340	0.02	0.0048	−0.0258	−0.0125	−0.1523	0.0088	0.0260	0.0289	0.0226
Sep 78	−0.0048	0.03	0.0093	0.0113	0.0129	−0.0394	0.0109	0.0056	−0.0508	0.0715
Oct 78	−0.0891	0.06	0.0355	0.0478	0.0384	0.1154	0.0543	0.0023	−0.1154	0.1282
Nov 78	0.0260	−0.09	−0.0273	−0.0588	−0.0640	−0.0463	−0.0089	−0.0261	0.0333	−0.0772
Dec 78	0.0172	0.05	0.0747	0.0558	0.0485	0.0521	0.1096	0.0441	0.0568	0.0317
Jan 79	0.0421	0.01	0.0843	0.0100	0.0120	0.0479	0.2273	−0.0491	−0.0656	−0.0337
Feb 79	−0.0284	−0.01	0.0579	0.0309	0.0268	0.1918	0.1276	−0.0430	−0.0585	−0.0301
Mar 79	0.0575	0.02	0.0612	−0.0092	−0.0390	0.0339	0.1316	−0.0254	−0.0889	0.0260
Apr 79	0.0036	0.00	0.0557	0.0198	0.0089	0.1509	0.1211	−0.0728	−0.1001	−0.0530
May 79	−0.0168	−0.02	−0.0271	0.0257	0.0229	0.1461	−0.0486	−0.0152	−0.0594	0.0155
Jun 79	0.0410	0.02	−0.0495	0.0599	0.0745	0.0278	−0.1076	−0.0010	−0.0210	0.0118

78   ©The Research Foundation of the ICFA

Table A.1.   (continued)

	S&P 500	EAFE	Composite	EMA	Europe	Africa	Latin America	Asia	East Asia	South Asia
Jul 79	0.0109	0.01	0.0135	0.0330	0.0385	0.0592	0.0187	−0.0221	−0.0353	−0.0138
Aug 79	0.0611	0.02	0.0797	−0.0529	−0.0756	0.0204	0.1115	0.1554	0.4484	−0.0238
Sep 79	0.0025	0.04	0.0138	−0.0091	−0.0411	0.0707	0.0209	0.0182	0.0063	0.0291
Oct 79	−0.0656	−0.02	−0.0466	−0.0141	−0.0229	0.0701	−0.0394	−0.0963	−0.1633	−0.0363
Nov 79	0.0514	0.01	0.0368	−0.0397	−0.0673	0.0062	0.0641	0.0424	0.1191	−0.0179
Dec 79	0.0192	0.03	0.0238	0.0045	−0.0275	0.0875	0.0519	−0.0355	−0.1211	0.0410
Jan 80	0.0610	0.05	−0.0050	0.0097	−0.0241	−0.0942	0.0063	−0.0535	−0.0987	−0.0190
Feb 80	0.0031	0.00	0.0477	0.0256	−0.0012	0.1063	0.0699	−0.0003	−0.0597	0.0401
Mar 80	−0.0987	−0.11	−0.0413	−0.0830	−0.1297	0.0777	−0.0384	−0.0055	0.0043	−0.0116
Apr 80	0.0429	0.10	0.0228	−0.0044	−0.0003	−0.0471	0.0111	0.0897	0.2204	0.0075
May 80	0.0562	0.05	0.0712	−0.0338	−0.0331	0.0262	0.1266	−0.0038	0.0051	−0.0106
Jun 80	0.0296	0.06	0.0112	0.0162	0.0010	−0.0111	0.0177	−0.0164	−0.0873	0.0395
Jul 80	0.0676	−0.01	−0.0290	−0.0056	−0.0177	0.0228	−0.0425	−0.0012	−0.0406	0.0262
Aug 80	0.0131	0.04	0.0127	0.0430	0.0189	0.2412	0.0095	−0.0040	−0.0506	0.0261
Sep 80	0.0281	0.04	−0.0365	0.0048	−0.0012	0.0749	−0.0458	−0.0433	−0.0958	−0.0116
Oct 80	0.0186	0.04	−0.0155	−0.0246	−0.0146	−0.0196	−0.0002	−0.0610	−0.1617	−0.0051
Nov 80	0.1095	−0.02	0.0088	−0.0547	−0.0784	−0.0218	0.0119	0.0645	0.0156	0.0877
Dec 80	−0.0315	0.01	0.0689	0.0056	−0.0331	−0.0039	0.1056	−0.0036	−0.0671	0.0246
Jan 81	−0.0438	−0.01	−0.0295	−0.1043	−0.1112	−0.0506	−0.0332	0.0551	0.2588	−0.0273
Feb 81	0.0208	−0.01	−0.0257	−0.0189	−0.0452	−0.0679	−0.0359	0.0065	−0.0895	0.0536
Mar 81	0.0380	0.04	−0.0140	0.0222	0.0129	−0.0223	−0.0447	0.0664	0.0532	0.0720
Apr 81	−0.0213	0.03	0.0336	0.0049	0.0359	−0.0722	0.0258	0.0809	0.1929	0.0342
May 81	0.0062	−0.04	−0.0885	−0.1214	−0.1631	−0.2262	−0.1016	−0.0251	0.0526	−0.0628
Jun 81	−0.0080	0.01	−0.0201	−0.0339	−0.0549	−0.0244	−0.0868	0.1753	0.3062	0.1037
Jul 81	0.0007	−0.04	−0.0770	0.0142	−0.0652	−0.0529	−0.1060	−0.0609	−0.0867	−0.0444
Aug 81	−0.0554	0.02	−0.0141	−0.0210	0.0042	−0.1756	0.0131	−0.0658	−0.0588	−0.0701
Sep 81	−0.0502	−0.10	−0.0813	0.0210	0.0022	−0.2791	−0.1331	−0.0253	−0.0939	0.0182
Oct 81	0.0528	0.02	−0.0436	0.0137	−0.0612	0.1363	−0.0693	−0.0277	−0.1117	0.0207
Nov 81	0.0441	0.11	0.0397	0.1344	0.1376	0.0478	−0.0031	0.0598	0.1063	0.0359
Dec 81	−0.0265	−0.01	0.0126	0.0117	−0.0188	−0.0906	0.0233	−0.0050	−0.0792	0.0362
Jan 82	−0.0163	−0.01	−0.0499	0.0278	−0.0130	−0.2323	−0.1134	0.0104	0.0907	−0.0294
Feb 82	−0.0512	−0.06	−0.0556	0.0513	0.0919	0.2100	−0.1543	0.0218	0.0392	0.0125
Mar 82	−0.0060	−0.05	−0.0708	−0.0483	−0.0629	−0.1009	−0.1164	−0.0306	−0.0125	−0.0402
Apr 82	0.0414	0.07	−0.0236	−0.0339	−0.0533	−0.0127	−0.0364	−0.0023	−0.0871	0.0442
May 82	−0.0288	−0.01	−0.0652	−0.0371	−0.0763	−0.1041	−0.1217	−0.0235	−0.1044	0.0159
Jun 82	−0.0174	−0.07	−0.0197	−0.0338	0.0357	−0.0960	−0.0249	−0.0056	0.1318	−0.0649
Jul 82	−0.0215	−0.01	−0.0475	−0.0179	0.0036	0.1025	−0.1197	0.0011	−0.0194	0.0118
Aug 82	0.1267	0.00	0.0129	0.0599	0.0900	0.0722	0.0198	−0.0209	−0.0494	−0.0063
Sep 82	0.0110	−0.01	0.0218	0.0125	0.0097	−0.0853	−0.0060	0.0492	−0.0334	0.0898
Oct 82	0.1126	0.00	−0.0448	−0.0485	−0.0581	0.0199	−0.0797	−0.0171	0.0268	−0.0366
Nov 82	0.0438	0.08	−0.0038	−0.0339	−0.0771	−0.0874	−0.0081	0.0172	0.0011	0.0248
Dec 82	0.0173	0.08	−0.0263	0.0798	0.1362	−0.1480	−0.2267	0.0446	0.0703	0.0328

Table A.1. (continued)

	S&P 500	EAFE	Composite	EMA	Europe	Africa	Latin America	Asia	East Asia	South Asia
Jan 83	0.0348	−0.01	−0.0865	−0.1205	−0.1852	−0.1880	−0.1174	−0.0518	−0.0308	−0.0620
Feb 83	0.0260	0.03	0.0097	−0.0063	−0.0495	0.1197	−0.0087	0.0270	0.0300	0.0256
Mar 83	0.0365	0.04	−0.0135	−0.0048	−0.0407	−0.0350	0.0300	−0.0376	−0.0383	−0.0372
Apr 83	0.0758	0.06	0.0201	−0.0300	−0.0474	0.0452	−0.0112	0.0626	0.1442	0.0235
May 83	−0.0052	−0.01	0.0192	−0.0426	−0.0757	0.1477	0.0376	0.0420	−0.0487	0.0906
Jun 83	0.0382	0.02	−0.0045	−0.0063	−0.0334	0.0912	0.0268	−0.0173	−0.0433	−0.0047
Jul 83	−0.0313	0.00	0.0146	−0.0256	−0.0124	−0.1202	0.0728	0.0064	0.0009	0.0090
Aug 83	0.0170	−0.02	−0.0008	0.0097	−0.0283	−0.0645	0.0120	−0.0115	−0.0599	0.0109
Sep 83	0.0136	0.04	0.0271	−0.0117	−0.0514	0.0575	0.1233	−0.0024	−0.0047	−0.0014
Oct 83	−0.0134	0.00	−0.0256	−0.0473	−0.0657	−0.0794	−0.0600	0.0023	0.0326	−0.0112
Nov 83	0.0233	0.02	−0.0225	−0.0184	−0.0532	−0.0142	−0.0247	−0.0231	−0.0537	−0.0086
Dec 83	−0.0061	0.04	0.0439	0.0151	−0.0861	−0.0191	0.0751	0.0403	0.0425	0.0393
Jan 84	−0.0065	0.05	0.0477	−0.0876	−0.1468	−0.1276	0.2332	0.0077	0.0962	−0.0322
Feb 84	−0.0328	0.01	0.0553	0.0278	0.0456	0.1216	0.1288	0.0199	0.0491	0.0062
Mar 84	0.0171	0.09	−0.0381	0.0352	0.0952	0.0040	−0.1229	−0.0073	0.0148	−0.0177
Apr 84	0.0069	−0.02	−0.0394	−0.0387	−0.0236	−0.0647	−0.0617	−0.0268	−0.0380	−0.0213
May 84	−0.0534	−0.10	0.0219	0.0028	−0.0122	0.0391	0.0985	−0.0145	−0.0565	0.0058
Jun 84	0.0221	0.00	−0.0134	−0.0172	−0.0065	−0.2516	−0.0654	0.0199	0.0193	0.0201
Jul 84	−0.0143	−0.06	0.002	−0.0079	0.0444	0.1222	−0.0440	0.0309	0.1049	−0.0053
Aug 84	0.1125	0.09	0.0151	−0.0084	−0.0127	−0.0183	0.0549	0.0020	−0.0124	0.0098
Sep 84	0.0002	−0.01	−0.0141	−0.0498	−0.0873	−0.0478	−0.0478	0.0157	−0.0208	0.0355
Oct 84	0.0026	0.03	−0.0340	−0.0168	−0.0440	−0.0077	−0.0999	−0.0055	−0.0301	0.0073
Nov 84	−0.0101	0.00	−0.0235	−0.0072	−0.0428	0.1037	−0.0240	−0.0281	0.0086	−0.0465
Dec 84	0.0253	0.02	0.0123	0.0407	0.0582	0.1387	−0.0490	0.0329	0.0608	0.0181
Jan 85	0.0768	0.02	0.0078	−0.0224	−0.0055	−0.0109	−0.0096	0.0155	−0.0138	0.0275
Feb 85	0.0137	−0.01	−0.0166	−0.0019	−0.0658	0.0082	0.0133	−0.0240	−0.0291	−0.0221
Mar 85	0.0018	0.08	0.0386	0.0266	0.0171	0.0026	0.0388	0.0403	−0.0134	0.0601
Apr 85	−0.0032	0.00	0.0080	0.0356	0.0720	0.0229	0.0196	0.0019	−0.0350	0.0145
May 85	0.0615	0.04	0.0206	0.0382	0.0397	0.0408	0.0006	0.0215	−0.0182	0.0344
Jun 85	0.0159	0.03	0.0099	0.0487	−0.0110	0.0160	0.0796	−0.0083	−0.0088	−0.0081
Jul 85	−0.0026	0.05	0.0157	0.0660	0.0315	0.0270	−0.0313	0.0165	−0.0731	0.0452
Aug 85	−0.0061	0.03	−0.0002	−0.0066	0.0310	−0.0066	0.2374	−0.0417	0.0309	−0.0623
Sep 85	−0.0321	0.06	0.0648	−0.0010	−0.0032	−0.0145	0.0498	0.0795	0.0634	0.0845
Oct 85	0.0447	0.07	0.0322	0.0485	−0.1687	0.0510	−0.0005	0.0370	0.1112	0.0143
Nov 85	0.0716	0.04	−0.0031	0.0075	0.1042	0.0047	0.0680	−0.0203	0.0777	−0.0530
Dec 85	0.0467	0.05	−0.0403	−0.0288	0.0200	−0.0336	−0.1432	−0.0179	0.1184	−0.0701
Jan 86	0.0044	0.03	0.0312	0.0340	0.1118	0.0570	0.0980	0.0173	0.0570	0.0003
Feb 86	0.0761	0.11	0.0363	0.0044	0.0748	0.0034	−0.0200	0.0534	0.1318	0.0142
Mar 86	0.0554	0.14	−0.0242	−0.0151	−0.0030	0.0072	−0.0256	−0.0253	0.0821	−0.0850
Apr 86	−0.0124	0.07	−0.0025	0.0475	−0.0012	0.0376	0.0599	−0.0226	−0.0253	−0.0209
May 86	0.0549	−0.04	0.0685	−0.0272	0.0075	−0.0125	0.1294	0.0702	0.1186	0.0440
Jun 86	0.0166	0.07	0.0414	−0.0115	0.1170	−0.0538	0.0553	0.0456	0.0342	0.0523

Table A.1.   (continued)

	S&P 500	EAFE	Composite	EMA	Europe	Africa	Latin America	Asia	East Asia	South Asia
Jul 86	−0.0569	0.06	0.0234	−0.0304	0.0874	−0.0624	0.0547	0.0236	0.0588	0.0034
Aug 86	0.0748	0.10	0.0065	0.0119	0.0909	0.0166	0.0159	0.0039	−0.0261	0.0220
Sep 86	−0.0822	−0.01	0.0313	0.0096	0.1538	−0.1240	0.0676	0.0259	0.0552	0.0090
Oct 86	0.0556	−0.07	0.0410	−0.1664	0.0754	−0.4887	0.0655	0.0605	0.0148	0.0885
Nov 86	0.0256	0.06	−0.0155	0.0067	−0.0434	0.0929	0.0783	−0.0390	0.0528	−0.0916
Dec 86	−0.0264	0.05	0.0485	0.0480	0.0798	0.0564	0.0992	0.0358	0.0375	0.0346
Jan 87	0.1343	0.11	0.0899	0.1790	0.3135	0.2123	0.1400	0.0650	0.0501	0.0755
Feb 87	0.0413	0.03	0.0736	0.0022	0.0365	−0.0993	0.0867	0.0799	0.0833	0.0775
Mar 87	0.0272	0.08	0.0339	0.0888	0.2013	−0.0858	0.0436	0.0238	0.1088	−0.0330
Apr 87	−0.0088	0.11	0.0976	0.1111	0.2224	−0.0928	0.0997	0.0951	0.1448	0.0572
May 87	0.0103	0.00	0.0569	0.1343	0.2169	−0.0129	0.0928	0.0351	0.0260	0.0427
Jun 87	0.0499	−0.03	0.0130	0.0182	−0.0025	0.2453	0.0470	0.0013	0.0091	−0.0050
Jul 87	0.0498	0.00	0.1621	0.2185	0.3137	−0.0272	0.2397	0.1266	0.1756	0.0863
Aug 87	0.0385	0.08	0.1122	0.2075	0.2721	−0.0488	0.1894	0.0659	0.1231	0.0147
Sep 87	−0.0220	−0.02	0.1510	0.3322	0.4062	−0.0061	0.0671	0.1455	0.3067	−0.0158
Oct 87	−0.2152	−0.14	−0.2546	−0.1611	−0.1863	0.0391	−0.3241	−0.2539	−0.2624	−0.2426
Nov 87	−0.0819	0.01	−0.0912	−0.1565	−0.1857	−0.0070	−0.3491	0.0150	0.0681	−0.0530
Dec 87	0.0738	0.03	−0.0507	−0.1304	−0.1703	0.0575	0.0263	−0.0474	−0.1141	0.0434
Jan 88	0.0427	0.02	0.1066	0.0109	0.0115	0.0131	0.1624	0.1158	0.1836	0.0423
Feb 88	0.0470	0.07	0.0823	−0.0972	−0.1203	−0.0174	0.1777	0.0923	0.1553	−0.0192
Mar 88	−0.0302	0.06	−0.0128	0.0016	−0.0034	0.0261	−0.0825	0.0008	−0.0092	0.0218
Apr 88	0.0108	0.02	0.0974	−0.0528	−0.0694	0.0274	−0.0546	0.1493	0.1708	0.1054
May 88	0.0078	−0.03	0.0752	−0.0294	−0.0381	−0.0032	0.1246	0.0793	0.0779	0.0822
Jun 88	0.0464	−0.03	0.0422	−0.0519	−0.0782	0.0310	0.0325	0.0523	0.0495	0.0598
Jul 88	−0.0040	0.03	0.1164	−0.0258	−0.0296	−0.0035	0.0229	0.1419	0.1884	0.0192
Aug 88	−0.0331	−0.07	0.0643	−0.0424	−0.0596	0.0714	0.0312	0.0773	0.1275	−0.0713
Sep 88	0.0424	0.04	0.0306	−0.0124	−0.0213	0.0012	0.0096	0.0357	0.0342	0.0420
Oct 88	0.0273	0.09	−0.1215	0.0276	0.0476	−0.0216	−0.0529	−0.1334	−0.1610	0.0058
Nov 88	−0.0142	0.06	0.0866	−0.0038	−0.0048	−0.0190	0.0882	0.0913	0.1104	0.0109
Dec 88	0.0181	0.01	−0.0922	−0.0550	−0.0733	0.0305	−0.0239	−0.1005	−0.1214	−0.0027
Jan 89	0.0723	0.02	0.0973	−0.0281	−0.0460	−0.0981	0.0339	0.1102	0.1204	0.0682
Feb 89	−0.0249	0.01	0.0567	0.0202	0.0523	0.0489	−0.0213	0.0658	0.0870	−0.0146
Mar 89	0.0236	−0.02	0.0695	−0.0187	−0.0131	−0.0312	0.0642	0.0743	0.0823	0.0410
Apr 89	0.0516	0.01	0.0336	0.0466	0.0476	0.0679	0.0560	0.0312	0.0208	0.0767
May 89	0.0402	−0.05	0.1328	0.0236	0.0352	−0.0069	0.1084	0.1396	0.1770	−0.0160
Jun 89	−0.0054	−0.02	−0.0175	0.0354	0.0338	0.0173	0.1926	−0.0362	−0.0495	0.0306
Jul 89	0.0898	0.13	0.0171	0.0767	0.0630	0.0583	−0.1241	0.0285	0.0335	0.0049
Aug 89	0.0193	−0.05	0.0272	0.0689	0.1129	0.0155	0.0838	0.0207	0.0222	0.0132
Sep 89	−0.0039	0.05	0.0403	0.3400	0.4248	0.0435	0.1441	0.0177	0.0132	0.0397
Oct 89	−0.0233	−0.04	−0.0119	−0.0013	−0.0100	0.0585	−0.0137	−0.0123	−0.0096	−0.0254
Nov 89	0.0208	0.05	−0.0504	−0.0307	−0.0403	0.0462	−0.0388	−0.0526	−0.0715	0.0387
Dec 89	0.0236	0.04	0.0593	0.0997	0.1167	0.0600	0.0585	0.0570	0.0465	0.1022

Table A.1. (continued)

	S&P 500	EAFE	Composite	EMA	Europe	Africa	Latin America	Asia	East Asia	South Asia
Jan 90	−0.0671	−0.04	0.1408	0.1437	0.1541	0.0277	−0.0407	0.1584	0.1994	−0.0197
Feb 90	0.0129	−0.07	−0.0279	0.0080	0.0066	0.0903	0.0781	−0.0378	−0.0476	0.0211
Mar 90	0.0263	−0.10	−0.0608	−0.0301	−0.0393	0.0212	0.0368	−0.0707	−0.0872	0.0202
Apr 90	−0.0247	−0.01	−0.1042	0.1712	0.1980	0.0142	0.0289	−0.1343	−0.1510	−0.0526
May 90	0.0975	0.11	−0.0444	0.0636	0.0668	0.0774	0.0984	−0.0692	−0.1078	0.0953
Jun 90	−0.0070	−0.01	−0.1098	0.1736	0.1900	0.1004	−0.0130	−0.1501	−0.1970	0.0101
Jul 90	−0.0032	0.01	0.0592	0.0733	0.0798	0.0634	0.0726	0.0553	0.0297	0.1244
Aug 90	−0.0903	−0.10	−0.1700	−0.0861	−0.0931	0.0469	−0.0576	−0.1983	−0.2531	−0.0642
Sep 90	−0.0492	−0.14	−0.1054	−0.0687	−0.0803	0.0284	−0.0347	−0.1234	−0.1343	−0.1023
Oct 90	−0.0037	0.16	0.0771	−0.0744	−0.0892	0.0395	0.0746	0.1032	0.1715	−0.0250
Nov 90	0.0644	−0.06	0.0502	−0.1328	−0.1579	0.0249	0.0599	0.0743	0.1406	−0.0731
Dec 90	0.0274	0.02	0.0292	−0.0132	−0.0195	0.0095	0.0485	0.0304	0.0311	0.0285
Jan 91	0.0442	0.03	−0.0439	0.0374	0.0473	−0.0184	0.0695	−0.0770	−0.1040	−0.0129
Feb 91	0.0716	0.11	0.1373	0.1267	0.1452	−0.0815	0.0975	0.1481	0.1597	0.1231
Mar 91	0.0238	−0.06	0.0015	−0.1305	−0.1512	0.0486	0.1037	0.0013	−0.0121	0.0304
Apr 91	0.0028	0.01	0.0399	−0.0978	−0.1179	0.0490	0.0622	0.0540	0.0787	0.0021
May 91	0.0428	0.01	−0.0021	−0.0740	−0.0843	0.0114	0.1349	−0.0255	−0.0418	0.0089
Jun 91	−0.0457	−0.07	−0.0124	−0.0701	−0.0788	−0.0283	0.0067	−0.0118	0.0052	−0.0456
Jul 91	0.0468	0.05	0.0193	−0.0328	−0.0302	−0.0485	0.0742	0.0075	0.0120	−0.0019
Aug 91	0.0235	−0.02	−0.0298	−0.0042	−0.0003	−0.0156	0.0583	−0.0631	−0.0758	−0.0365
Sep 91	−0.0164	0.06	0.0136	−0.0736	−0.0894	−0.0010	0.0154	0.0224	0.0488	−0.0309
Oct 91	0.0134	0.01	−0.0117	−0.0311	−0.0375	0.0105	0.0840	−0.0461	−0.0647	−0.0055
Nov 91	−0.0404	−0.05	−0.0135	0.0672	0.0850	−0.0410	−0.0411	−0.0097	−0.0304	0.0329
Dec 91	0.1143	0.05	0.0420	0.0523	0.0557	0.0087	0.0892	0.0215	0.0007	0.0614
Jan 92	−0.0186	−0.02	0.1093	0.0306	0.0357	−0.0100	0.0977	0.1241	0.1408	0.0942
Feb 92	0.0128	−0.04	0.0034	−0.1179	−0.1317	−0.0674	0.0797	−0.0200	−0.0803	0.0899
Mar 92	−0.0196	−0.07	−0.0021	−0.0354	−0.0079	−0.3615	0.0103	−0.0055	−0.0762	0.1031
Apr 92	0.0291	0.01	−0.0141	−0.0138	−0.0215	−0.0041	0.0179	−0.0320	−0.0254	−0.0406
May 92	0.0054	0.07	−0.0294	−0.0618	−0.0710	0.0376	0.0121	−0.0501	−0.0299	−0.0767
Jun 92	−0.0145	−0.05	−0.0288	0.1311	0.1500	0.0011	−0.1352	0.0242	0.0117	0.0413
Jul 92	0.0403	−0.03	−0.0426	−0.0356	−0.0368	−0.0147	−0.0064	−0.0622	−0.0849	−0.0322
Aug 92	−0.0202	0.06	−0.0215	−0.0184	−0.0267	0.0708	−0.0648	0.0020	0.0036	0.0001
Sep 92	0.0115	−0.02	−0.0256	−0.0799	−0.0961	−0.0236	−0.0558	−0.0053	−0.0749	0.0811
Oct 92	0.0036	−0.05	0.0523	−0.1349	−0.1576	−0.0027	0.0384	0.0752	0.1167	0.0317
Nov 92	0.0337	0.01	−0.0064	−0.0054	−0.0159	0.0431	−0.0279	0.0042	0.0452	−0.0419
Dec 92	0.0131	0.01	0.0059	0.0059	0.0107	−0.1208	0.0691	−0.0233	−0.0348	−0.0091
Jan 93	0.0073	0.00	0.0102	0.0659	0.0687	0.0276	−0.0116	0.0166	0.0092	0.0264
Feb 93	0.0135	0.03	0.0501	0.1389	0.1770	−0.2020	−0.0005	0.0677	0.1399	−0.0080
Mar 93	0.0215	0.09	0.0099	−0.0437	−0.0485	−0.0598	0.0574	−0.0067	0.0286	−0.0496
Apr 93	−0.0245	0.10	0.0275	0.2131	0.2218	0.3592	−0.0392	0.0447	0.0343	0.0585
May 93	0.0270	0.02	−0.0021	−0.0001	−0.0047	−0.0544	0.0165	−0.0102	−0.0432	0.0328
Jun 93	0.0033	−0.02	0.0128	0.0755	0.0760	0.0340	0.0966	−0.0290	−0.0616	0.0101

Table A.1.   (continued)

	S&P 500	EAFE	Composite	EMA	Europe	Africa	Latin America	Asia	East Asia	South Asia
Jul 93	−0.0047	0.04	0.0154	−0.0346	−0.0409	0.0760	0.0137	0.0210	−0.0158	0.0621
Aug 93	0.0381	0.05	0.0415	0.1318	0.1515	0.0857	0.0671	0.0207	−0.0360	0.0798
Sep 93	−0.0074	−0.02	0.0311	0.0912	0.1004	−0.0461	0.0227	0.0294	0.0188	0.0393
Oct 93	0.0203	0.03	0.0750	−0.0138	−0.0161	0.0489	0.0433	0.1006	0.0538	0.1435
Nov 93	−0.0094	−0.01	0.0692	0.0718	0.0816	0.0541	0.0809	0.0633	0.0680	0.0593
Dec 93	0.0123	0.07	0.1822	0.0620	0.0614	0.0861	0.1202	0.2239	0.2630	0.1902
Jan 94	0.0335	0.09	0.0342	0.0034	−0.0164	0.4508	0.1517	−0.0175	0.0350	−0.0651
Feb 94	−0.0270	0.00	−0.0325	−0.0585	−0.1218	−0.0339	−0.0296	−0.0276	−0.0644	0.0068
Mar 94	−0.0435	−0.04	−0.0793	−0.0538	−0.1310	−0.0255	−0.0632	−0.0940	−0.0581	−0.1252
Apr 94	0.0130	0.04	0.0181	0.0822	−0.1277	0.1594	−0.0802	0.0537	0.0639	0.0441
May 94	0.0163	−0.01	0.0190	−0.0168	−0.0334	−0.0133	0.0441	0.0162	0.0207	0.0118
Jun 94	−0.0247	0.01	−0.0194	0.0258	0.0936	0.0093	−0.0693	−0.0060	−0.0115	−0.0009
Jul 94	0.0331	0.01	0.0597	0.0705	0.0789	0.0710	0.0768	0.0492	0.0585	0.0405
Aug 94	0.0407	0.02	0.1147	0.0665	0.0624	0.0694	0.1853	0.0941	0.0838	0.1040
Sep 94	−0.0241	−0.03	0.0318	0.0170	−0.0079	0.0243	0.0523	0.0251	0.0663	−0.0138
Oct 94	0.0229	0.03	−0.0136	0.0559	−0.0002	0.0727	−0.0336	−0.0203	−0.0395	−0.0003
Nov 94	−0.0367	−0.05	−0.0375	0.0057	0.0518	−0.0057	−0.0188	−0.0584	−0.0344	−0.0827
Dec 94	0.0146	0.01	−0.0461	0.0105	−0.0354	0.0232	−0.1664	0.0010	0.0306	−0.0301
Jan 95	0.0243	−0.04	−0.1163	−0.1393	−0.0881	−0.1549	−0.1321	−0.1030	−0.1094	−0.0959
Feb 95	0.0361	0.00	−0.0020	0.0730	0.0655	0.0767	−0.1369	0.0334	0.0005	0.0665
Mar 95	0.0273	0.06	0.0155	0.1172	0.1487	0.1112	−0.0358	0.0065	0.0363	−0.0215
Apr 95	0.0280	0.04	0.0151	0.0360	0.0510	0.0306	0.1535	−0.0349	−0.0526	−0.0172
May 95	0.0363	−0.01	0.0407	−0.0155	0.0083	−0.0252	0.0219	0.0645	0.0170	0.1103
Jun 95	0.0213	−0.02	−0.0043	0.0131	0.0358	0.0074	0.0131	−0.0155	−0.0232	−0.0088

Table A.2. EMA, Europe, and Jordan: Total Value-Weighted Stock Returns, January 1976–June 1995

	EMA	Europe	Greece	Hungary	Poland	Portugal	Turkey	Jordan
Jan 76	0.0623	0.0603	0.0603					
Feb 76	−0.0247	−0.0159	−0.0159					
Mar 76	−0.0402	−0.0417	−0.0417					
Apr 76	0.0127	0.0149	0.0149					
May 76	−0.0661	−0.0619	−0.0619					
Jun 76	0.0341	0.0268	0.0268					
Jul 76	−0.0177	−0.0160	−0.0160					
Aug 76	0.0034	0.0147	0.0147					
Sep 76	−0.0067	−0.0330	−0.0330					
Oct 76	−0.0140	−0.0010	−0.0010					
Nov 76	0.0117	0.0226	0.0226					
Dec 76	−0.0004	0.0076	0.0076					
Jan 77	−0.0390	−0.0287	−0.0287					
Feb 77	−0.0120	0.0003	0.0003					
Mar 77	0.1079	0.1093	0.1093					
Apr 77	0.1013	0.116	0.1160					
May 77	−0.0504	−0.0533	−0.0533					
Jun 77	0.0867	0.0891	0.0891					
Jul 77	0.0257	0.0328	0.0328					
Aug 77	0.0766	0.0837	0.0837					
Sep 77	−0.0275	−0.0281	−0.0281					
Oct 77	−0.0805	−0.0845	−0.0845					
Nov 77	0.0327	0.0296	0.0296					
Dec 77	0.0742	0.0657	0.0657					
Jan 78	0.0146	0.0179	0.0179					
Feb 78	−0.0057	−0.0079	−0.0079					0.0279
Mar 78	−0.0103	−0.0096	−0.0096					0.0091
Apr 78	0.0203	−0.0078	−0.0078					0.2443
May 78	0.0101	0.0051	0.0051					0.0515
Jun 78	0.0053	0.0097	0.0097					−0.0077
Jul 78	0.0094	0.0008	0.0008					−0.0053
Aug 78	−0.0258	−0.0125	−0.0125					−0.0413
Sep 78	0.0113	0.0129	0.0129					0.0200
Oct 78	0.0478	0.0384	0.0384					0.0720
Nov 78	−0.0588	−0.0640	−0.0640					−0.0385
Dec 78	0.0558	0.0485	0.0485					0.0898
Jan 79	0.0100	0.0120	0.0120					−0.0111
Feb 79	0.0309	0.0268	0.0268					−0.0019
Mar 79	−0.0092	−0.0390	−0.0390					0.1166
Apr 79	0.0198	0.0089	0.0089					0.0175
May 79	0.0257	0.0229	0.0229					−0.0111
Jun 79	0.0599	0.0745	0.0745					0.0097

Table A.2.   (continued)

	EMA	Europe	Greece	Hungary	Poland	Portugal	Turkey	Jordan
Jul 79	0.0330	0.0385	0.0385					−0.0039
Aug 79	−0.0529	−0.0756	−0.0756					0.0179
Sep 79	−0.0091	−0.0411	−0.0411					0.0886
Oct 79	−0.0141	−0.0229	−0.0229					−0.0205
Nov 79	−0.0397	−0.0673	−0.0673					0.0395
Dec 79	0.0045	−0.0275	−0.0275					0.0688
Jan 80	0.0097	−0.0241	−0.0241					0.1638
Feb 80	0.0256	−0.0012	−0.0012					0.0629
Mar 80	−0.0830	−0.1297	−0.1297					−0.0353
Apr 80	−0.0044	−0.0003	−0.0003					0.0058
May 80	−0.0338	−0.0331	−0.0331					−0.0602
Jun 80	0.0162	0.0010	0.0010					0.0623
Jul 80	−0.0056	−0.0177	−0.0177					0.0068
Aug 80	0.0430	0.0189	0.0189					0.0053
Sep 80	0.0048	−0.0012	−0.0012					−0.0199
Oct 80	−0.0246	−0.0146	−0.0146					−0.0477
Nov 80	−0.0547	−0.0784	−0.0784					−0.0244
Dec 80	0.0056	−0.0331	−0.0331					0.0875
Jan 81	−0.1043	−0.1112	−0.1112					−0.1213
Feb 81	−0.0189	−0.0452	−0.0452					0.0570
Mar 81	0.0222	0.0129	0.0129					0.0600
Apr 81	0.0049	0.0359	0.0359					−0.0078
May 81	−0.1214	−0.1631	−0.1631					−0.0096
Jun 81	−0.0339	−0.0549	−0.0549					−0.0087
Jul 81	0.0142	−0.0652	−0.0652					0.1319
Aug 81	−0.0210	0.0042	0.0042					−0.0064
Sep 81	0.0210	0.0022	0.0022					0.1024
Oct 81	0.0137	−0.0612	−0.0612					0.0659
Nov 81	0.1344	0.1376	0.1376					0.1444
Dec 81	0.0117	−0.0188	−0.0188					0.0496
Jan 82	0.0278	−0.0130	−0.0130					0.0889
Feb 82	0.0513	0.0919	0.0919					0.0102
Mar 82	−0.0483	−0.0629	−0.0629					−0.0323
Apr 82	−0.0339	−0.0533	−0.0533					−0.0216
May 82	−0.0371	−0.0763	−0.0763					−0.0037
Jun 82	−0.0338	0.0357	0.0357					−0.0739
Jul 82	−0.0179	0.0036	0.0036					−0.0415
Aug 82	0.0599	0.0900	0.0900					0.0377
Sep 82	0.0125	0.0097	0.0097					0.0225
Oct 82	−0.0485	−0.0581	−0.0581					−0.0465
Nov 82	−0.0339	−0.0771	−0.0771					0.0015
Dec 82	0.0798	0.1362	0.1362					0.0579

Table A.2.   (continued)

	EMA	Europe	Greece	Hungary	Poland	Portugal	Turkey	Jordan
Jan 83	−0.1205	−0.1852	−0.1852					−0.0686
Feb 83	−0.0063	−0.0495	−0.0495					0.0155
Mar 83	−0.0048	−0.0407	−0.0407					0.0186
Apr 83	−0.0300	−0.0474	−0.0474					−0.0239
May 83	−0.0426	−0.0757	−0.0757					−0.0343
Jun 83	−0.0063	−0.0334	−0.0334					0.0020
Jul 83	−0.0256	−0.0124	−0.0124					−0.0255
Aug 83	0.0097	−0.0283	−0.0283					0.0324
Sep 83	−0.0117	−0.0514	−0.0514					0.0025
Oct 83	−0.0473	−0.0657	−0.0657					−0.0376
Nov 83	−0.0184	−0.0532	−0.0532					−0.0042
Dec 83	0.0151	−0.0861	−0.0861					0.0567
Jan 84	−0.0876	−0.1468	−0.1468					−0.0634
Feb 84	0.0278	0.0456	0.0456					0.0173
Mar 84	0.0352	0.0952	0.0952					0.0157
Apr 84	−0.0387	−0.0236	−0.0236					−0.0431
May 84	0.0028	−0.0122	−0.0122					0.0067
Jun 84	−0.0172	−0.0065	−0.0065					−0.0096
Jul 84	−0.0079	0.0444	0.0444					−0.0302
Aug 84	−0.0084	−0.0127	−0.0127					−0.0064
Sep 84	−0.0498	−0.0873	−0.0873					−0.0364
Oct 84	−0.0168	−0.0440	−0.0440					−0.0078
Nov 84	−0.0072	−0.0428	−0.0428					0.0005
Dec 84	0.0407	0.0582	0.0582					0.0312
Jan 85	−0.0224	−0.0055	−0.0055					−0.0487
Feb 85	−0.0019	−0.0658	−0.0658					0.0015
Mar 85	0.0266	0.0171	0.0171					0.0741
Apr 85	0.0356	0.0720	0.0720					0.0463
May 85	0.0382	0.0397	0.0397					0.0335
Jun 85	0.0487	−0.0110	−0.0110					0.1218
Jul 85	0.0660	0.0315	0.0315					0.1326
Aug 85	−0.0066	0.0310	0.0310					−0.0151
Sep 85	−0.0010	−0.0032	−0.0032					0.0178
Oct 85	0.0485	−0.1687	−0.1687					0.0946
Nov 85	0.0075	0.1042	0.1042					−0.0058
Dec 85	−0.0288	0.0200	0.0200					−0.0323
Jan 86	0.0340	0.1118	0.1118					−0.0113
Feb 86	0.0044	0.0748	0.0893			0.0425		−0.0179
Mar 86	−0.0151	−0.0030	−0.1234			0.2767		−0.0499
Apr 86	0.0475	−0.0012	−0.0750			0.1141		0.0806
May 86	−0.0272	0.0075	0.0561			−0.0556		−0.0596
Jun 86	−0.0115	0.1170	0.0586			0.1815		−0.0064

Table A.2.   (continued)

	EMA	Europe	Greece	Hungary	Poland	Portugal	Turkey	Jordan
Jul 86	−0.0304	0.0874	0.0841			0.0905		−0.0434
Aug 86	0.0119	0.0909	0.0700			0.1098		−0.0371
Sep 86	0.0096	0.1538	0.1382			0.1674		0.0997
Oct 86	−0.1664	0.0754	0.0289			0.1078		−0.0001
Nov 86	0.0067	−0.0434	−0.0296			−0.0500		0.0073
Dec 86	0.0480	0.0798	0.0519			0.0935		0.0148
Jan 87	0.179	0.3135	0.3094			0.3491	0.2333	−0.0206
Feb 87	0.0022	0.0365	−0.0075			0.0538	0.0539	0.0159
Mar 87	0.0888	0.2013	0.2634			0.2496	−0.0066	−0.0089
Apr 87	0.1111	0.2224	−0.0803			0.3699	0.2528	−0.0218
May 87	0.1343	0.2169	−0.0431			0.2472	0.4359	−0.0229
Jun 87	0.0182	−0.0025	0.1096			−0.1170	0.2776	−0.0372
Jul 87	0.2185	0.3137	0.1636			0.2272	0.6940	−0.0154
Aug 87	0.2075	0.2721	0.2305			0.3578	0.1635	0.0072
Sep 87	0.3322	0.4062	0.3806			0.7084	−0.1663	0.0042
Oct 87	−0.1611	−0.1863	−0.1205			−0.2067	−0.1929	−0.0041
Nov 87	−0.1565	−0.1857	−0.1516			−0.2930	0.2460	0.0151
Dec 87	−0.1304	−0.1703	0.0674			−0.2426	−0.2528	0.0446
Jan 88	0.0109	0.0115	−0.3081			0.0991	0.2933	0.0055
Feb 88	−0.0972	−0.1203	0.0090			−0.1474	−0.1709	−0.0123
Mar 88	0.0016	−0.0034	−0.0184			0.0484	−0.1078	0.0119
Apr 88	−0.0528	−0.0694	−0.0077			−0.0902	−0.0841	−0.0205
May 88	−0.0294	−0.0381	−0.0716			−0.0495	0.0404	−0.0105
Jun 88	−0.0519	−0.0782	−0.0522			−0.0528	−0.1748	0.0008
Jul 88	−0.0258	−0.0296	−0.0103			−0.0581	0.0337	−0.0251
Aug 88	−0.0424	−0.0596	−0.0125			−0.0277	−0.2566	−0.0351
Sep 88	−0.0124	−0.0213	0.0108			−0.0388	−0.0581	0.0144
Oct 88	0.0276	0.0476	0.0526			0.0884	−0.1195	−0.0196
Nov 88	−0.0038	−0.0048	−0.0390			0.0372	−0.0650	0.0095
Dec 88	−0.0550	−0.0733	−0.0199			−0.1047	−0.1312	−0.0286
Jan 89	−0.0281	−0.0460	−0.0870			−0.0093	−0.0501	0.0824
Feb 89	0.0202	0.0523	0.0038			0.0433	0.2587	−0.1281
Mar 89	−0.0187	−0.0131	−0.0165			−0.0066	−0.0350	−0.0405
Apr 89	0.0466	0.0476	0.0313			0.0197	0.2245	0.0291
May 89	0.0236	0.0352	0.1390			−0.0811	0.3048	−0.0216
Jun 89	0.0354	0.0338	−0.0051			−0.0257	0.2951	0.0546
Jul 89	0.0767	0.0630	0.1352			0.0896	−0.1116	0.1615
Aug 89	0.0689	0.1129	0.1027			0.0968	0.1803	−0.1223
Sep 89	0.3400	0.4248	0.4288			0.2902	0.7870	−0.0198
Oct 89	−0.0013	−0.0100	−0.0116			−0.0610	0.0938	0.0413
Nov 89	−0.0307	−0.0403	−0.0463			0.0094	−0.1173	0.0040
Dec 89	0.0997	0.1167	0.0121			0.0012	0.4941	−0.0158

Table A.2. (continued)

	EMA	Europe	Greece	Hungary	Poland	Portugal	Turkey	Jordan
Jan 90	0.1437	0.1541	0.1658			−0.0590	0.4062	0.1256
Feb 90	0.0080	0.0066	0.0462			−0.0078	−0.0087	−0.0511
Mar 90	−0.0301	−0.0393	0.0544			−0.0407	−0.1132	0.0209
Apr 90	0.1712	0.1980	0.5855			0.0235	0.0328	0.0345
May 90	0.0636	0.0668	0.0474			0.0211	0.1503	0.0082
Jun 90	0.1736	0.1900	0.4374			−0.0079	0.0681	0.0272
Jul 90	0.0733	0.0798	0.0153			−0.0073	0.2866	−0.0192
Aug 90	−0.0861	−0.0931	−0.1041			−0.0786	−0.0882	−0.1285
Sep 90	−0.0687	−0.0803	−0.1184			−0.1093	−0.0020	0.0003
Oct 90	−0.0744	−0.0892	−0.1274			0.0343	−0.1268	0.0037
Nov 90	−0.1328	−0.1579	−0.0864			−0.0806	−0.3145	0.0075
Dec 90	−0.0132	−0.0195	0.0406			−0.0424	−0.0969	0.0323
Jan 91	0.0374	0.0473	−0.0141			0.0495	0.0905	−0.0625
Feb 91	0.1267	0.1452	0.3289			0.1399	0.0290	0.0818
Mar 91	−0.1305	−0.1512	−0.1117			−0.1153	−0.2004	0.0862
Apr 91	−0.0978	−0.1179	−0.1215			−0.0027	−0.1725	0.0606
May 91	−0.0740	−0.0843	−0.1342			−0.0248	−0.0695	−0.0337
Jun 91	−0.0701	−0.0788	−0.0976			−0.0623	−0.0715	−0.0009
Jul 91	−0.0328	−0.0302	0.0333			0.0584	−0.1390	−0.0479
Aug 91	−0.0042	−0.0003	0.0608			−0.0129	−0.0554	−0.0443
Sep 91	−0.0736	−0.0894	−0.1386			0.0116	−0.1103	0.0622
Oct 91	−0.0311	−0.0375	0.0116			−0.0372	−0.0947	−0.0067
Nov 91	0.0672	0.0850	0.0269			−0.0717	0.3105	−0.0013
Dec 91	0.0523	0.0557	0.0146			0.1179	0.0551	0.0628
Jan 92	0.0306	0.0357	0.1041			−0.0675	0.0434	0.0115
Feb 92	−0.1179	−0.1317	−0.0356			−0.0257	−0.3003	0.0127
Mar 92	−0.0354	−0.0079	−0.0781			0.0481	0.0407	−0.0027
Apr 92	−0.0138	−0.0215	0.0078			0.0557	−0.1318	0.0720
May 92	−0.0618	−0.0710	−0.0820			0.0208	−0.1569	−0.0265
Jun 92	0.1311	0.1500	0.1581			0.0438	0.2805	0.0268
Jul 92	−0.0356	−0.0368	−0.0277			0.0120	−0.1031	−0.0358
Aug 92	−0.0184	−0.0267	−0.0281			−0.0175	−0.0366	0.0159
Sep 92	−0.0799	−0.0961	−0.1492			−0.0623	−0.0611	0.0578
Oct 92	−0.1349	−0.1576	−0.1723			−0.1418	−0.1584	−0.0087
Nov 92	−0.0054	−0.0159	0.0218			−0.0491	−0.0216	0.0456
Dec 92	0.0059	0.0107	0.0168			−0.0135	0.0336	0.0549
Jan 93	0.0659	0.0687	0.0891	−0.0867	0.0088	0.0508	0.0850	0.0658
Feb 93	0.1389	0.1770	0.0833	−0.0232	0.0022	0.0366	0.3971	−0.0347
Mar 93	−0.0437	−0.0485	−0.0753	−0.0372	0.1875	0.0030	−0.0692	0.0202
Apr 93	0.2131	0.2218	−0.0329	−0.0360	0.4000	0.0190	0.5378	0.0569
May 93	−0.0001	−0.0047	0.0263	0.0245	0.9921	0.0834	−0.0797	0.0892
Jun 93	0.0755	0.0760	−0.0247	0.0077	−0.1073	−0.0370	0.1918	0.0897

Table A.2.   (continued)

	EMA	Europe	Greece	Hungary	Poland	Portugal	Turkey	Jordan
Jul 93	−0.0346	−0.0409	0.0972	0.0800	0.1346	−0.0121	−0.1137	−0.0128
Aug 93	0.1318	0.1515	0.0385	0.1975	0.3298	0.2016	0.1698	−0.0610
Sep 93	0.0912	0.1004	−0.0562	0.0515	0.0346	−0.0377	0.2398	0.0439
Oct 93	−0.0138	−0.0161	0.0006	0.0450	0.2190	0.0445	−0.0564	−0.0140
Nov 93	0.0718	0.0816	−0.0158	0.0069	0.1298	−0.0178	0.1567	−0.0563
Dec 93	0.0620	0.0614	0.0497	0.0318	0.3527	0.0302	0.0612	0.0583
Jan 94	0.0034	−0.0164	0.1403	0.6601	0.2362	0.1319	−0.1532	0.0314
Feb 94	−0.0585	−0.1218	0.0171	−0.1509	0.1966	0.0257	−0.2727	0.0050
Mar 94	−0.0538	−0.1310	−0.0493	−0.0272	−0.3061	0.0380	−0.2602	−0.0104
Apr 94	0.0822	−0.1277	0.0052	−0.0882	−0.2549	−0.0198	−0.3074	−0.0578
May 94	−0.0168	−0.0334	−0.1274	−0.0423	0.0218	−0.0943	0.1364	0.0137
Jun 94	0.0258	0.0936	0.0126	−0.0744	−0.2499	−0.0227	0.3561	−0.0022
Jul 94	0.0705	0.0789	0.0099	0.0651	0.1653	0.0473	0.1373	−0.0332
Aug 94	0.0665	0.0624	0.0096	0.0122	0.0748	0.0781	0.0820	−0.0040
Sep 94	0.0170	−0.0079	0.0188	−0.0572	−0.1475	−0.0051	−0.0063	−0.0041
Oct 94	0.0559	−0.0002	−0.0112	0.0224	−0.0962	0.0380	−0.0121	−0.0282
Nov 94	0.0057	0.0518	−0.0025	−0.0728	−0.0196	−0.0124	0.1415	−0.0014
Dec 94	0.0105	−0.0354	0.0412	−0.0874	−0.0724	−0.0139	−0.0792	−0.0172
Jan 95	−0.1393	−0.0881	−0.0581	−0.2275	−0.1750	−0.0783	−0.0968	0.0044
Feb 95	0.0730	0.0655	0.0284	−0.0015	0.0443	0.0593	0.0981	0.0118
Mar 95	0.1172	0.1487	0.0861	−0.0268	−0.0460	0.0692	0.2653	−0.0064
Apr 95	0.0360	0.0510	0.0039	0.1274	0.4038	0.0303	0.0547	0.0808
May 95	−0.0155	0.0083	0.0626	0.0164	−0.1160	−0.0114	0.0067	0.0856
Jun 95	0.0131	0.0358	0.0465	−0.0032	0.0951	0.0011	0.0434	−0.0387

Note: Blanks in columns indicate market was not yet covered by the IFC Emerging Markets Data Base (EMDB).

Table A.3. Africa: Total Value-Weighted Stock Returns, January 1976–June 1995

	Africa	Nigeria	South Africa	Zimbabwe
Jan 76	0.0779			0.0779
Feb 76	−0.0924			−0.0924
Mar 76	−0.0281			−0.0281
Apr 76	−0.0054			−0.0054
May 76	−0.0998			−0.0998
Jun 76	0.0921			0.0921
Jul 76	−0.0299			−0.0299
Aug 76	−0.0842			−0.0842
Sep 76	0.2282			0.2282
Oct 76	−0.1052			−0.1052
Nov 76	−0.0594			−0.0594
Dec 76	−0.0576			−0.0576
Jan 77	−0.1180			−0.1180
Feb 77	−0.1162			−0.1162
Mar 77	0.0935			0.0935
Apr 77	−0.0412			−0.0412
May 77	−0.0168			−0.0168
Jun 77	0.0606			0.0606
Jul 77	−0.0536			−0.0536
Aug 77	−0.0109			−0.0109
Sep 77	−0.0193			−0.0193
Oct 77	−0.0261			−0.0261
Nov 77	0.0733			0.0733
Dec 77	0.1794			0.1794
Jan 78	−0.0222			−0.0222
Feb 78	−0.0397			−0.0397
Mar 78	−0.0562			−0.0562
Apr 78	−0.0880			−0.0880
May 78	−0.0374			−0.0374
Jun 78	−0.0165			−0.0165
Jul 78	0.1842			0.1842
Aug 78	−0.1523			−0.1523
Sep 78	−0.0394			−0.0394
Oct 78	0.1154			0.1154
Nov 78	−0.0463			−0.0463
Dec 78	0.0521			0.0521
Jan 79	0.0479			0.0479
Feb 79	0.1918			0.1918
Mar 79	0.0339			0.0339
Apr 79	0.1509			0.1509
May 79	0.1461			0.1461
Jun 79	0.0278			0.0278

Table A.3.   (continued)

	Africa	Nigeria	South Africa	Zimbabwe
Jul 79	0.0592			0.0592
Aug 79	0.0204			0.0204
Sep 79	0.0707			0.0707
Oct 79	0.0701			0.0701
Nov 79	0.0062			0.0062
Dec 79	0.0875			0.0875
Jan 80	−0.0942			−0.0942
Feb 80	0.1063			0.1063
Mar 80	0.0777			0.0777
Apr 80	−0.0471			−0.0471
May 80	0.0262			0.0262
Jun 80	−0.0111			−0.0111
Jul 80	0.0228			0.0228
Aug 80	0.2412			0.2412
Sep 80	0.0749			0.0749
Oct 80	−0.0196			−0.0196
Nov 80	−0.0218			−0.0218
Dec 80	−0.0039			−0.0039
Jan 81	−0.0506			−0.0506
Feb 81	−0.0679			−0.0679
Mar 81	−0.0223			−0.0223
Apr 81	−0.0722			−0.0722
May 81	−0.2262			−0.2262
Jun 81	−0.0244			−0.0244
Jul 81	−0.0529			−0.0529
Aug 81	−0.1756			−0.1756
Sep 81	−0.2791			−0.2791
Oct 81	0.1363			0.1363
Nov 81	0.0478			0.0478
Dec 81	−0.0906			−0.0906
Jan 82	−0.2323			−0.2323
Feb 82	0.2100			0.2100
Mar 82	−0.1009			−0.1009
Apr 82	−0.0127			−0.0127
May 82	−0.1041			−0.1041
Jun 82	−0.0960			−0.0960
Jul 82	0.1025			0.1025
Aug 82	0.0722			0.0722
Sep 82	−0.0853			−0.0853
Oct 82	0.0199			0.0199
Nov 82	−0.0874			−0.0874
Dec 82	−0.1480			−0.1480

Table A.3.   (continued)

	Africa	Nigeria	South Africa	Zimbabwe
Jan 83	−0.1880			−0.1880
Feb 83	0.1197			0.1197
Mar 83	−0.0350			−0.0350
Apr 83	0.0452			0.0452
May 83	0.1477			0.1477
Jun 83	0.0912			0.0912
Jul 83	−0.1202			−0.1202
Aug 83	−0.0645			−0.0645
Sep 83	0.0575			0.0575
Oct 83	−0.0794			−0.0794
Nov 83	−0.0142			−0.0142
Dec 83	−0.0191			−0.0191
Jan 84	−0.1276			−0.1276
Feb 84	0.1216			0.1216
Mar 84	0.0040			0.0040
Apr 84	−0.0647			−0.0647
May 84	0.0391			0.0391
Jun 84	−0.2516			−0.2516
Jul 84	0.1222			0.1222
Aug 84	−0.0183			−0.0183
Sep 84	−0.0478			−0.0478
Oct 84	−0.0077			−0.0077
Nov 84	0.1037			0.1037
Dec 84	0.1387			0.1387
Jan 85	−0.0109	−0.0174		0.2439
Feb 85	0.0082	0.0024		0.1094
Mar 85	0.0026	−0.0094		0.1932
Apr 85	0.0229	0.0200		0.0614
May 85	0.0408	0.0072		0.4598
Jun 85	0.0160	0.0093		0.0731
Jul 85	0.0270	0.0355		−0.0418
Aug 85	−0.0066	−0.0003		−0.0608
Sep 85	−0.0145	−0.0213		0.0497
Oct 85	0.0510	0.0522		0.0406
Nov 85	0.0047	0.0048		0.0034
Dec 85	−0.0336	−0.0312		−0.0544
Jan 86	0.0570	0.0505		0.1145
Feb 86	0.0034	0.0046		−0.0069
Mar 86	0.0072	0.0186		−0.0887
Apr 86	0.0376	0.0407		0.0090
May 86	−0.0125	−0.0069		−0.0653
Jun 86	−0.0538	−0.0674		0.0837

Table A.3. (continued)

	Africa	Nigeria	South Africa	Zimbabwe
Jul 86	−0.0624	−0.0737		0.0398
Aug 86	0.0166	0.0260		−0.0581
Sep 86	−0.1240	−0.1551		0.1483
Oct 86	−0.4887	−0.5605		−0.0310
Nov 86	0.0929	0.1233		0.0037
Dec 86	0.0564	0.0584		0.0498
Jan 87	0.2123	0.2447		0.1034
Feb 87	−0.0993	−0.1143		−0.0449
Mar 87	−0.0858	−0.1250		0.0476
Apr 87	−0.0928	−0.1816		0.1623
May 87	−0.0129	−0.0485		0.0594
Jun 87	0.2453	0.3887		−0.0191
Jul 87	−0.0272	−0.0466		0.0244
Aug 87	−0.0488	−0.0700		0.0042
Sep 87	−0.0061	−0.0436		0.0802
Oct 87	0.0391	−0.0004		0.1197
Nov 87	−0.0070	−0.0407		0.0547
Dec 87	0.0575	0.0247		0.1120
Jan 88	0.0131	−0.0172		0.0599
Feb 88	−0.0174	−0.0038		−0.0370
Mar 88	0.0261	0.0114		0.0480
Apr 88	0.0274	0.0768		−0.0424
May 88	−0.0032	−0.0014		−0.0059
Jun 88	0.0310	0.0380		0.0203
Jul 88	−0.0035	−0.0347		0.0473
Aug 88	0.0714	0.0834		0.0532
Sep 88	0.0012	0.0236		−0.0335
Oct 88	−0.0216	−0.0264		−0.0138
Nov 88	−0.0190	−0.0859		0.0891
Dec 88	0.0305	0.0166		0.0495
Jan 89	−0.0981	−0.1986		0.0322
Feb 89	0.0489	−0.0073		0.1044
Mar 89	−0.0312	−0.0027		−0.0564
Apr 89	0.0679	0.0524		0.0825
May 89	−0.0069	0.0174		−0.0292
Jun 89	0.0173	0.0576		−0.0203
Jul 89	0.0583	0.0333		0.0843
Aug 89	0.0155	0.0508		−0.0192
Sep 89	0.0435	0.0603		0.0258
Oct 89	0.0585	0.0750		0.0403
Nov 89	0.0462	0.0361		0.0578
Dec 89	0.0600	0.0610		0.0588

Table A.3.   (continued)

	Africa	Nigeria	South Africa	Zimbabwe
Jan 90	0.0277	0.0302		0.0248
Feb 90	0.0903	0.0354		0.1503
Mar 90	0.0212	0.0119		0.0303
Apr 90	0.0142	0.0188		0.0096
May 90	0.0774	0.0898		0.0654
Jun 90	0.1004	0.0901		0.1100
Jul 90	0.0634	0.0261		0.0973
Aug 90	0.0469	0.0220		0.0682
Sep 90	0.0284	0.0156		0.0387
Oct 90	0.0395	0.0339		0.0440
Nov 90	0.0249	−0.0252		0.0637
Dec 90	0.0095	0.0318		−0.0059
Jan 91	−0.0184	−0.0225		−0.0156
Feb 91	−0.0815	0.0162		−0.1499
Mar 91	0.0486	0.0754		0.0265
Apr 91	0.0490	0.0079		0.0846
May 91	0.0114	0.0307		−0.0041
Jun 91	−0.0283	−0.0257		−0.0304
Jul 91	−0.0485	−0.0576		−0.0411
Aug 91	−0.0156	0.1021		−0.1099
Sep 91	−0.0010	0.1877		−0.1853
Oct 91	0.0105	0.0183		−0.0003
Nov 91	−0.0410	0.0954		−0.2314
Dec 91	0.0087	0.0202		−0.0123
Jan 92	−0.0100	0.0551		−0.1336
Feb 92	−0.0674	−0.0865		−0.0237
Mar 92	−0.3615	−0.4229		−0.2305
Apr 92	−0.0041	0.0180		−0.0395
May 92	0.0376	0.0355		0.0410
Jun 92	0.0011	0.0639		−0.1007
Jul 92	−0.0147	−0.0080		−0.0276
Aug 92	0.0708	0.0826		0.0475
Sep 92	−0.0236	0.0205		−0.1143
Oct 92	−0.0027	0.0356		−0.0942
Nov 92	0.0431	0.0872		−0.0770
Dec 92	−0.1208	−0.1304		−0.0899
Jan 93	0.0276	0.0525		−0.0492
Feb 93	−0.2020	−0.2856		0.0080
Mar 93	−0.0598	−0.0875		−0.0105
Apr 93	0.3592	0.5826		0.0209
May 93	−0.0544	−0.0959		0.0416
Jun 93	0.0340	0.0405		0.0208

Table A.3. (continued)

	Africa	Nigeria	South Africa	Zimbabwe
Jul 93	0.0760	−0.0011		0.2323
Aug 93	0.0857	0.0170		0.1982
Sep 93	−0.0461	−0.1507		0.0981
Oct 93	0.0489	−0.0643		0.1708
Nov 93	0.0541	0.0845		0.0281
Dec 93	0.0861	−0.0256		0.1874
Jan 94	0.4508	1.00_3		0.0349
Feb 94	−0.0339	0.0398	−0.0385	0.3022
Mar 94	−0.0255	0.0599	−0.0267	−0.0322
Apr 94	0.1594	0.0406	0.1637	0.0042
May 94	−0.0133	0.0379	−0.0157	0.1143
Jun 94	0.0093	0.0267	0.0113	−0.1490
Jul 94	0.0710	0.0110	0.0727	0.0048
Aug 94	0.0694	0.0001	0.0701	0.0963
Sep 94	0.0243	0.0175	0.0242	0.0461
Oct 94	0.0727	0.0590	0.0738	−0.0076
Nov 94	−0.0057	0.0588	−0.0065	−0.0082
Dec 94	0.0232	0.0452	0.0241	−0.0887
Jan 95	−0.1549	0.0431	−0.1599	0.0691
Feb 95	0.0767	0.0564	0.0796	−0.1263
Mar 95	0.1112	−0.7014	0.1271	−0.0483
Apr 95	0.0306	0.1051	0.0299	0.0784
May 95	−0.0252	0.1826	−0.0274	0.1098
Jun 95	0.0074	0.2324	0.0056	0.0618

Note: Blanks in columns indicate market was not yet covered by the EMDB.

Table A.4. Latin America: Total Value-Weighted Stock Returns, January 1976–June 1995

	Latin America	Argentina	Brazil	Chile	Colombia	Mexico	Peru	Venezuela
Jan 76	−0.0185	0.0386	0.1791	−0.1307		0.0113		
Feb 76	0.0219	1.1033	−0.0096	0.1752		0.0058		
Mar 76	0.0845	−0.0023	−0.1162	−0.0852		0.1052		
Apr 76	0.0361	0.3863	−0.0468	0.2870		0.0103		
May 76	−0.0329	0.9877	0.1351	−0.0315		−0.0331		
Jun 76	0.0465	0.4886	0.1337	0.3517		0.0070		
Jul 76	0.0410	0.4135	−0.0828	0.2726		0.0003		
Aug 76	−0.0149	0.6161	0.0260	0.0430		−0.0278		
Sep 76	−0.2196	−0.2727	−0.0702	0.0988		−0.2944		
Oct 76	−0.2129	−0.0822	−0.1925	−0.0983		−0.2552		
Nov 76	0.0817	−0.6218	0.2044	−0.1443		0.1823		
Dec 76	0.1565	0.0836	−0.0714	0.1825		0.1482		
Jan 77	−0.0974	−0.0368	0.0691	−0.0415		−0.1144		
Feb 77	0.0282	0.2263	−0.0306	0.0179		0.0315		
Mar 77	0.1168	0.0471	0.0612	0.3287		0.0500		
Apr 77	0.0650	−0.1371	−0.0304	0.2326		0.0010		
May 77	0.0849	−0.1102	−0.0627	0.3114		−0.0221		
Jun 77	0.0568	−0.1368	−0.0447	0.1496		−0.0015		
Jul 77	0.0951	−0.1238	−0.0138	0.2032		0.0168		
Aug 77	−0.0714	−0.0901	0.0610	−0.1596		0.0042		
Sep 77	0.0270	−0.1156	0.1023	0.0211		0.0312		
Oct 77	0.0346	−0.2296	−0.0345	−0.1370		0.1572		
Nov 77	0.0686	0.2977	−0.0954	−0.0475		0.1304		
Dec 77	0.0861	−0.1743	−0.0859	0.1580		0.0517		
Jan 78	0.1080	0.1359	0.0705	0.0376		0.1448		
Feb 78	0.2795	0.1229	0.0593	0.6286		0.1161		
Mar 78	−0.0105	0.1839	0.0452	−0.0769		0.0346		
Apr 78	0.1023	−0.0968	−0.0767	0.1045		0.1010		
May 78	0.0157	−0.0753	−0.0088	−0.0155		0.0355		
Jun 78	0.0182	0.0841	−0.0568	−0.0945		0.0870		
Jul 78	−0.0019	0.3214	0.0309	−0.0201		0.0073		
Aug 78	0.0088	0.0958	−0.0268	−0.0111		0.0186		
Sep 78	0.0109	0.7921	−0.0296	−0.0556		0.0368		
Oct 78	0.0543	−0.1572	−0.0731	0.0787		0.0456		
Nov 78	−0.0089	−0.0660	−0.0779	−0.0403		0.0025		
Dec 78	0.1096	−0.0399	−0.0409	0.0348		0.1353		
Jan 79	0.2273	0.6092	−0.0833	0.2179		0.2303		
Feb 79	0.1276	0.1301	−0.0626	0.0014		0.1664		
Mar 79	0.1316	0.1847	−0.0485	0.0356		0.1558		
Apr 79	0.1211	0.3247	0.1079	−0.0023		0.1489		
May 79	−0.0486	0.5206	−0.0285	−0.0178		−0.0546		
Jun 79	−0.1076	−0.1465	−0.0663	−0.0753		−0.1141		

Table A.4. (continued)

	Latin America	Argentina	Brazil	Chile	Colombia	Mexico	Peru	Venezuela
Jul 79	0.0187	0.0179	−0.0073	0.0086		0.0208		
Aug 79	0.1115	0.0250	−0.0158	0.2513		0.0827		
Sep 79	0.0209	−0.1795	0.1222	0.1439		−0.0082		
Oct 79	−0.0394	0.2633	0.1871	0.2400		−0.1156		
Nov 79	0.0641	−0.1275	−0.1812	0.0153		0.0826		
Dec 79	0.0519	0.0100	−0.1970	0.1174		0.0286		
Jan 80	0.0063	0.1572	0.1887	−0.0085		0.0120		
Feb 80	0.0699	0.5908	0.0892	0.2040		0.0203		
Mar 80	−0.0384	−0.0735	−0.0587	0.2455		−0.1621		
Apr 80	0.0111	−0.1695	−0.0331	0.0625		−0.0220		
May 80	0.1266	−0.2013	0.1852	0.1119		0.1371		
Jun 80	0.0177	0.0306	0.1833	0.0953		−0.0363		
Jul 80	−0.0425	0.0066	−0.0228	−0.0354		−0.0481		
Aug 80	0.0095	−0.0137	−0.0324	−0.0089		0.0243		
Sep 80	−0.0458	−0.0265	−0.1383	0.0015		−0.0826		
Oct 80	−0.0002	−0.1814	−0.1163	−0.0523		0.0441		
Nov 80	0.0119	0.0583	−0.0909	−0.0416		0.0531		
Dec 80	0.1056	−0.0826	−0.1049	0.0856		0.1195		
Jan 81	−0.0332	0.1565	0.0261	−0.1029		0.0141		
Feb 81	−0.0359	−0.0718	0.0064	−0.0112		−0.0505		
Mar 81	−0.0447	0.1828	−0.1566	−0.0448		−0.0446		
Apr 81	0.0258	−0.4502	0.0539	0.1433		−0.0461		
May 81	−0.1016	−0.2765	0.1420	−0.1461		−0.0692		
Jun 81	−0.0868	0.0923	0.0516	−0.0728		−0.0964		
Jul 81	−0.1060	−0.0618	0.0251	−0.1616		−0.0672		
Aug 81	0.0131	−0.2202	0.0670	0.1254		−0.0579		
Sep 81	−0.1331	−0.0632	0.0644	−0.1912		−0.0893		
Oct 81	−0.0693	−0.0605	0.2117	0.0010		−0.1165		
Nov 81	−0.0031	0.3743	0.0706	−0.0396		0.0246		
Dec 81	0.0233	−0.0466	−0.1919	0.0329		0.0163		
Jan 82	−0.1134	−0.3699	0.2989	−0.0684		−0.1462		
Feb 82	−0.1543	−0.0845	0.0829	0.0645		−0.3278		
Mar 82	−0.1164	−0.2363	−0.0415	−0.1428		−0.0822		
Apr 82	−0.0364	0.0416	−0.0064	0.1035		−0.2069		
May 82	−0.1217	0.1974	0.1926	−0.0882		−0.1791		
June 82	−0.0249	0.3358	−0.0106	−0.1071		0.1335		
July 82	−0.1197	−0.2728	−0.0514	−0.1258		−0.1102		
Aug 82	0.0198	−0.1816	−0.0375	−0.0268		0.0922		
Sep 82	−0.0060	−0.1218	−0.1737	−0.0887		0.1433		
Oct 82	−0.0797	−0.0241	−0.0089	−0.1151		−0.0284		
Nov 82	−0.0081	0.0014	−0.2025	−0.1263		0.1540		
Dec 82	−0.2267	0.0369	−0.0861	0.0006		−0.4663		

Table A.4. (continued)

	Latin America	Argentina	Brazil	Chile	Colombia	Mexico	Peru	Venezuela
Jan 83	−0.1174	0.1585	0.3543	−0.2803		0.2015		
Feb 83	−0.0087	0.0183	−0.1997	−0.0575		0.0472		
Mar 83	0.0300	0.0581	−0.0699	0.1348		−0.0779		
Apr 83	−0.0112	0.3445	−0.0256	−0.0481		0.0364		
May 83	0.0376	0.0758	−0.0853	−0.0553		0.1478		
Jun 83	0.0268	−0.2207	0.0830	−0.1232		0.1749		
Jul 83	0.0728	0.0730	−0.1747	0.0985		0.0537		
Aug 83	0.0120	0.2148	−0.0428	0.0600		−0.0249		
Sep 83	0.1233	−0.0240	0.1565	0.0008		0.2267		
Oct 83	−0.0600	0.2498	0.2334	−0.0573		−0.0619		
Nov 83	−0.0247	−0.0196	0.1432	0.0088		−0.0479		
Dec 83	0.0751	−0.3246	0.2312	0.0181		0.1175		
Jan 84	0.2332	0.3873	−0.1042	0.1338		0.3012		
Feb 84	0.1288	0.1608	−0.1674	0.0847		0.1543		
Mar 84	−0.1229	0.2888	−0.0691	−0.0265		−0.1752		
Apr 84	−0.0617	−0.4097	0.2259	0.0485		−0.1329		
May 84	0.0985	0.0501	0.0483	0.0633		0.1258		
Jun 84	−0.0654	0.0360	−0.0588	−0.0406		−0.0837		
Jul 84	−0.0440	−0.3213	0.0143	−0.0879		−0.0100		
Aug 84	0.0549	0.0342	0.1221	−0.0374		0.1209		
Sep 84	−0.0478	−0.1990	−0.0551	−0.1695		0.0263		
Oct 84	−0.0999	−0.2348	0.0878	−0.0845		−0.1076		
Nov 84	−0.0240	0.2930	0.4389	−0.0644		−0.0039		
Dec 84	−0.0490	0.1011	0.0854	−0.0458		−0.0505		
Jan 85	−0.0096	−0.2085	−0.1689	0.0789	0.0021	−0.0832		0.0196
Feb 85	0.0133	0.0181	0.0316	−0.0927	0.0088	0.0717		0.0311
Mar 85	0.0388	−0.2091	−0.1130	0.1195	−0.0074	0.0162		0.0271
Apr 85	0.0196	−0.3159	−0.0780	0.0383	−0.0210	0.0207		0.0189
May 85	0.0006	−0.0849	0.2068	0.0671	−0.0469	−0.0572		0.0432
Jun 85	0.0796	0.016	0.3315	−0.0083	−0.0068	0.0224		0.0198
Jul 85	−0.0313	0.0270	0.0905	−0.0943	−0.0079	−0.1287		0.0479
Aug 85	0.2374	−0.0066	0.1766	0.0433	−0.0198	0.1632		0.0223
Sep 85	0.0498	−0.0145	0.1971	0.1346	−0.0933	0.0142		0.0142
Oct 85	−0.0005	0.0510	0.2245	0.0115	−0.0056	0.1963		0.0323
Nov 85	0.0680	0.0047	0.0370	0.0638	0.0611	0.0664		0.1134
Dec 85	−0.1432	−0.0336	−0.1164	0.0666	0.0262	−0.0851		−0.4978
Jan 86	0.0980	0.0570	−0.1562	0.1040	0.1456	0.1813		−0.0550
Feb 86	−0.0200	0.0034	−0.0284	0.1512	0.0978	−0.0403		−0.0861
Mar 86	−0.0256	0.0072	0.5753	0.0923	0.0862	−0.1370		0.0343
Apr 86	0.0599	0.0376	0.2526	0.0429	0.0715	−0.1416		0.1592
May 86	0.1294	−0.0125	−0.0074	0.0943	0.1171	0.1620		0.1383
Jun 86	0.0553	−0.0538	−0.0785	0.0984	−0.0242	0.0342		0.2936

Table A.4. (continued)

	Latin America	Argentina	Brazil	Chile	Colombia	Mexico	Peru	Venezuela
Jul 86	0.0547	−0.0624	−0.0513	0.0900	0.0153	0.1296		−0.1476
Aug 86	0.0159	0.0166	−0.1387	−0.0333	0.0535	0.0653		0.0116
Sep 86	0.0676	−0.1240	−0.1876	0.0505	0.0806	0.1688		0.0707
Oct 86	0.0655	−0.4887	0.0948	−0.0054	0.0679	0.1556		−0.0047
Nov 86	0.0783	0.0929	−0.2152	0.1092	0.1665	0.1087		0.0086
Dec 86	0.0992	0.0564	−0.1064	0.1989	0.0884	0.0491		0.1138
Jan 87	0.1400	0.2123	−0.2736	0.0073	0.1199	0.1788		0.1514
Feb 87	0.0867	−0.0993	−0.2210	0.0582	−0.0325	0.2547		0.1870
Mar 87	0.0436	−0.0858	−0.0639	−0.0705	−0.0783	0.1506		0.0229
Apr 87	0.0997	−0.0928	0.1017	−0.0003	0.0446	0.1998		−0.0297
May 87	0.0928	−0.0129	−0.2857	−0.0312	0.0277	0.1521		0.1379
Jun 87	0.0470	0.2453	0.1632	0.0723	0.0421	0.0551		−0.0471
Jul 87	0.2397	−0.0272	0.1308	0.2185	0.1033	0.3341		−0.0582
Aug 87	0.1894	−0.0488	−0.1876	0.1995	0.0610	0.2012		−0.0571
Sep 87	0.0671	−0.0061	0.1489	0.1128	0.2289	0.0885		−0.0121
Oct 87	−0.3241	0.0391	−0.1979	−0.1907	0.0176	−0.4247		0.0511
Nov 87	−0.3491	−0.0070	−0.0511	−0.1235	−0.0156	−0.5932		0.1560
Dec 87	0.0263	0.0575	−0.0519	0.0917	0.1091	−0.0485		−0.0269
Jan 88	0.1624	0.0131	0.3182	0.0640	−0.0225	0.3960		0.0627
Feb 88	0.1777	−0.0174	−0.0993	0.0562	−0.0265	0.3934		0.0718
Mar 88	−0.0825	0.0261	0.5262	−0.0418	−0.0167	−0.1283		−0.0488
Apr 88	−0.0546	0.0274	0.1331	−0.0476	−0.0304	−0.1043		0.0098
May 88	0.1246	−0.0032	0.1054	−0.0185	−0.0174	0.2559		−0.0928
Jun 88	0.0325	0.0310	−0.1152	0.2090	−0.0332	−0.0104		−0.1158
Jul 88	0.0229	−0.0035	−0.1512	0.0218	−0.0226	0.0075		−0.0776
Aug 88	0.0312	0.0714	0.0095	0.0564	0.0017	0.0306		−0.0439
Sep 88	0.0096	0.0012	0.1492	0.0086	0.0385	−0.0049		−0.0556
Oct 88	−0.0529	−0.0216	−0.0209	−0.0723	−0.0097	−0.0060		−0.0163
Nov 88	0.0882	−0.0190	−0.0373	0.0699	0.0097	0.1521		−0.0102
Dec 88	−0.0239	0.0305	0.2104	0.0374	0.0004	−0.0676		0.0658
Jan 89	0.0339	−0.0981	−0.2213	0.1074	0.0337	0.0012		0.1042
Feb 89	−0.0213	0.0489	0.4315	0.0912	0.0551	−0.0455		−0.2334
Mar 89	0.0642	−0.0312	0.3361	0.0047	−0.0171	0.0849		0.1078
Apr 89	0.0560	0.0679	0.4782	0.0945	−0.0252	0.0995		−0.2388
May 89	0.1084	−0.0069	−0.0921	0.0385	0.0419	0.1461		−0.0832
Jun 89	0.1926	0.0173	−0.4306	−0.0648	−0.0163	0.1357		−0.0221
Jul 89	−0.1241	0.0583	0.1355	−0.0610	0.0082	0.0149		−0.0003
Aug 89	0.0838	0.0155	−0.0845	−0.0337	−0.0359	0.0934		0.1115
Sep 89	0.1441	0.0435	0.0786	0.0554	−0.0380	0.0696		0.0104
Oct 89	−0.0137	0.0585	0.1705	0.0980	0.0642	−0.0427		0.0579
Nov 89	−0.0388	0.0462	−0.2382	0.0270	0.0100	−0.0378		−0.1206
Dec 89	0.0585	0.0600	0.2298	0.0859	0.0624	0.0664		−0.0034

Table A.4. (continued)

	Latin America	Argentina	Brazil	Chile	Colombia	Mexico	Peru	Venezuela
Jan 90	−0.0407	0.0277	0.0101	0.0577	0.0048	0.0290		−0.0876
Feb 90	0.0781	0.0903	1.1794	0.1410	0.0999	0.0424		0.1645
Mar 90	0.0368	0.0212	−0.6892	0.0067	0.0214	0.0103		0.4897
Apr 90	0.0289	0.0142	0.3831	−0.0203	0.0160	0.0304		0.1786
May 90	0.0984	0.0774	−0.1998	−0.0444	0.0286	0.1816		0.0803
Jun 90	−0.0130	0.1004	−0.0331	0.0527	0.2104	−0.0489		0.0088
Jul 90	0.0726	0.0634	0.2734	−0.0072	0.0421	0.0814		0.2937
Aug 90	−0.0576	0.0469	−0.2023	−0.0440	−0.0889	−0.0976		0.4583
Sep 90	−0.0347	0.0284	−0.1374	−0.0100	−0.0606	−0.0893		0.1816
Oct 90	0.0746	0.0395	−0.1617	−0.0314	0.0292	0.1223		0.1593
Nov 90	0.0599	0.0249	−0.0139	0.1335	0.0507	0.0281		0.1268
Dec 90	0.0485	0.0095	−0.1112	0.1353	0.0041	0.0122		0.1881
Jan 91	0.0695	−0.0184	0.4176	0.1506	−0.0103	−0.0190		0.1833
Feb 91	0.0975	−0.0815	0.3414	0.2114	0.0519	0.0466		−0.0623
Mar 91	0.1037	0.0486	−0.1124	0.0284	−0.0346	0.1911		0.0023
Apr 91	0.0622	0.0490	0.0632	0.0053	−0.0257	0.1203		−0.0284
May 91	0.1349	0.0114	0.3430	0.0473	0.0615	0.2027		−0.0499
Jun 91	0.0067	−0.0283	0.0154	0.1433	0.0690	−0.0266		−0.0698
Jul 91	0.0742	−0.0485	0.0454	0.1148	−0.0023	0.0895		−0.0287
Aug 91	0.0583	−0.0156	−0.1171	0.0788	−0.0106	0.0414		−0.0231
Sep 91	0.0154	−0.0010	−0.0946	0.0907	0.0453	−0.0129		0.1004
Oct 91	0.0840	0.0105	0.0613	−0.0643	0.3426	0.0971		0.2925
Nov 91	−0.0411	−0.0410	−0.2532	−0.0597	0.3729	0.0162		−0.0141
Dec 91	0.0892	0.0087	0.4042	0.0012	0.3732	0.0323		0.1241
Jan 92	0.0977	−0.0100	0.2547	0.0158	0.3325	0.0882		0.1327
Feb 92	0.0797	−0.0674	−0.0199	0.1758	−0.1747	0.1484		−0.0529
Mar 92	0.0103	−0.3615	0.0461	0.0947	−0.0743	−0.0118		−0.2602
Apr 92	0.0179	−0.0041	0.0405	0.0152	0.0503	−0.0222		0.0762
May 92	0.0121	0.0376	−0.0249	0.0060	0.0614	0.0111		−0.0779
Jun 92	−0.1352	0.0011	−0.2774	0.0212	0.1536	−0.1421		−0.0056
Jul 92	−0.0064	−0.0147	0.0462	−0.0114	0.1537	−0.0040		−0.0021
Aug 92	−0.0648	0.0708	−0.0130	−0.0907	−0.0156	−0.0653		0.0991
Sep 92	−0.0558	−0.0236	0.0353	−0.0721	−0.0216	−0.0553		−0.2066
Oct 92	0.0384	−0.0027	−0.1460	0.0864	−0.0318	0.1584		−0.0941
Nov 92	−0.0279	0.0431	−0.1527	−0.0802	−0.0431	0.0606		−0.1042
Dec 92	0.0691	−0.1208	0.1447	0.0271	0.0293	0.0474		0.0360
Jan 93	−0.0116	0.0276	−0.0507	0.1260	−0.0607	−0.0459	0.2501	−0.1306
Feb 93	−0.0005	−0.2020	0.2557	−0.0602	−0.0538	−0.0541	−0.2930	0.0096
Mar 93	0.0574	−0.0598	0.0060	−0.0486	−0.0816	0.1283	0.1027	−0.1291
Apr 93	−0.0392	0.3592	−0.0200	−0.0883	0.0052	−0.0470	−0.0554	0.1567
May 93	0.0165	−0.0544	0.1252	0.0134	0.1017	−0.0294	−0.0773	0.0659
Jun 93	0.0966	0.0340	0.2315	0.1359	0.0262	0.0291	0.1756	0.0210

100

Table A.4. (continued)

	Latin America	Argentina	Brazil	Chile	Colombia	Mexico	Peru	Venezuela
Jul 93	0.0137	0.0760	−0.0209	−0.0365	0.0324	0.0553	0.0307	−0.0519
Aug 93	0.0671	0.0857	0.0677	0.0485	0.1094	0.0696	0.1425	−0.1269
Sep 93	0.0227	−0.0461	0.0872	0.0230	0.0691	−0.0296	0.0265	0.0428
Oct 93	0.0433	0.0489	−0.0771	0.0414	0.0744	0.1030	0.1315	0.1241
Nov 93	0.0809	0.0541	0.1130	0.0612	0.0478	0.1115	−0.1772	−0.0450
Dec 93	0.1202	0.0861	−0.0003	0.1150	0.1649	0.1687	0.2144	0.0531
Jan 94	0.1517	0.4508	0.2923	0.2033	0.1822	0.0807	0.1663	−0.0271
Feb 94	−0.0296	−0.0339	0.0404	−0.0169	0.1726	−0.0918	0.0858	0.2198
Mar 94	−0.0632	−0.0255	0.0209	−0.1476	0.0904	−0.1001	−0.0398	−0.0621
Apr 94	−0.0802	0.1594	−0.2077	0.0737	−0.0356	−0.0344	−0.0393	−0.2238
May 94	0.0441	−0.0133	−0.0221	0.0952	−0.0125	0.0663	0.0682	0.0193
Jun 94	−0.0693	0.0093	−0.0240	−0.0223	0.0005	−0.0971	−0.0748	−0.2536
Jul 94	0.0768	0.0710	0.1599	−0.0118	0.0140	0.0695	−0.0490	0.0216
Aug 94	0.1853	0.0694	0.4140	0.1505	−0.0930	0.0956	0.0816	0.1804
Sep 94	0.0523	0.0243	0.1042	0.0518	0.0179	0.0153	0.2616	0.0442
Oct 94	−0.0336	0.0727	−0.0455	0.1099	−0.0611	−0.0667	0.0420	−0.0284
Nov 94	−0.0188	−0.0057	−0.0281	−0.0210	−0.0751	0.0083	−0.0461	−0.1641
Dec 94	−0.1664	0.0232	−0.0563	−0.0468	0.0508	−0.3502	−0.0015	0.1076
Jan 95	−0.1321	−0.1549	−0.0753	−0.0335	0.1184	−0.3177	−0.1773	−0.0580
Feb 95	−0.1369	0.0767	−0.1609	−0.0343	−0.0649	−0.1801	−0.0645	−0.0927
Mar 95	−0.0358	0.1112	−0.1127	0.0056	−0.1061	0.0232	0.0372	−0.0069
Apr 95	0.1535	0.0306	0.1925	0.0985	−0.0585	0.2136	0.3204	−0.0051
May 95	0.0219	−0.0252	0.0073	0.1246	−0.0181	−0.0473	0.0286	−0.0067
Jun 95	0.0131	0.0074	−0.0380	0.0227	0.1102	0.1025	0.0019	−0.0021

Note: Blanks in columns indicate market was not yet covered by the EMDB.

Table A.5.   Asia and East Asia: Total Value-Weighted Stock Returns, January 1976–June 1995

	Asia	East Asia	China	Korea	Philippines	Taiwan
Jan 76	0.1683	0.2687		0.2687		
Feb 76	−0.0039	0.0047		0.0047		
Mar 76	0.0027	0.0611		0.0611		
Apr 76	−0.0053	−0.0008		−0.0008		
May 76	−0.0448	−0.0385		−0.0385		
Jun 76	0.0614	0.0580		0.0580		
Jul 76	0.0316	−0.0024		−0.0024		
Aug 76	0.0203	−0.0376		−0.0376		
Sep 76	0.0282	0.0131		0.0131		
Oct 76	0.0067	0.0743		0.0743		
Nov 76	−0.0005	0.0337		0.0337		
Dec 76	0.0729	0.1216		0.1216		
Jan 77	0.0528	0.1051		0.1051		
Feb 77	0.0322	0.0477		0.0477		
Mar 77	0.0345	−0.0005		−0.0005		
Apr 77	−0.0105	−0.0539		−0.0539		
May 77	0.0335	0.0478		0.0478		
Jun 77	0.0205	0.0424		0.0424		
Jul 77	0.0121	−0.0122		−0.0122		
Aug 77	0.0966	0.0629		0.0629		
Sep 77	0.0688	0.2008		0.2008		
Oct 77	0.0994	0.0804		0.0804		
Nov 77	−0.0490	−0.0259		−0.0259		
Dec 77	0.0868	0.1107		0.1107		
Jan 78	0.0935	0.1246		0.1246		
Feb 78	0.0247	0.0489		0.0489		
Mar 78	0.0076	0.0013		0.0013		
Apr 78	0.0161	0.0426		0.0426		
May 78	0.0405	0.0544		0.0544		
Jun 78	0.0348	0.0516		0.0516		
Jul 78	0.0303	0.0513		0.0513		
Aug 78	0.0260	0.0289		0.0289		
Sep 78	0.0056	−0.0508		−0.0508		
Oct 78	0.0023	−0.1154		−0.1154		
Nov 78	−0.0261	0.0333		0.0333		
Dec 78	0.0441	0.0568		0.0568		
Jan 79	−0.0491	−0.0656		−0.0656		
Feb 79	−0.0430	−0.0585		−0.0585		
Mar 79	−0.0254	−0.0889		−0.0889		
Apr 79	−0.0728	−0.1001		−0.1001		
May 79	−0.0152	−0.0594		−0.0594		
Jun 79	−0.0010	−0.0210		−0.0210		

Table A.5. (continued)

	Asia	East Asia	China	Korea	Philippines	Taiwan
Jul 79	−0.0221	−0.0353		−0.0353		
Aug 79	0.1554	0.4484		0.4484		
Sep 79	0.0182	0.0063		0.0063		
Oct 79	−0.0963	−0.1633		−0.1633		
Nov 79	0.0424	0.1191		0.1191		
Dec 79	−0.0355	−0.1211		−0.1211		
Jan 80	−0.0535	−0.0987		−0.0987		
Feb 80	−0.0003	−0.0597		−0.0597		
Mar 80	−0.0055	0.0043		0.0043		
Apr 80	0.0897	0.2204		0.2204		
May 80	−0.0038	0.0051		0.0051		
Jun 80	−0.0164	−0.0873		−0.0873		
Jul 80	−0.0012	−0.0406		−0.0406		
Aug 80	−0.0040	−0.0506		−0.0506		
Sep 80	−0.0433	−0.0958		−0.0958		
Oct 80	−0.0610	−0.1617		−0.1617		
Nov 80	0.0645	0.0156		0.0156		
Dec 80	−0.0036	−0.0671		−0.0671		
Jan 81	0.0551	0.2588		0.2588		
Feb 81	0.0065	−0.0895		−0.0895		
Mar 81	0.0664	0.0532		0.0532		
Apr 81	0.0809	0.1929		0.1929		
May 81	−0.0251	0.0526		0.0526		
Jun 81	0.1753	0.3062		0.3062		
Jul 81	−0.0609	−0.0867		−0.0867		
Aug 81	−0.0658	−0.0588		−0.0588		
Sep 81	−0.0253	−0.0939		−0.0939		
Oct 81	−0.0277	−0.1117		−0.1117		
Nov 81	0.0598	0.1063		0.1063		
Dec 81	−0.0050	−0.0792		−0.0792		
Jan 82	0.0104	0.0907		0.0907		
Feb 82	0.0218	0.0392		0.0392		
Mar 82	−0.0306	−0.0125		−0.0125		
Apr 82	−0.0023	−0.0871		−0.0871		
May 82	−0.0235	−0.1044		−0.1044		
Jun 82	−0.0056	0.1318		0.1318		
Jul 82	0.0011	−0.0194		−0.0194		
Aug 82	−0.0209	−0.0494		−0.0494		
Sep 82	0.0492	−0.0334		−0.0334		
Oct 82	−0.0171	0.0268		0.0268		
Nov 82	0.0172	0.0011		0.0011		
Dec 82	0.0446	0.0703		0.0703		

Table A.5.   (continued)

	Asia	East Asia	China	Korea	Philippines	Taiwan
Jan 83	−0.0518	−0.0308		−0.0308		
Feb 83	0.0270	0.0300		0.0300		
Mar 83	−0.0376	−0.0383		−0.0383		
Apr 83	0.0626	0.1442		0.1442		
May 83	0.0420	−0.0487		−0.0487		
Jun 83	−0.0173	−0.0433		−0.0433		
Jul 83	0.0064	0.0009		0.0009		
Aug 83	−0.0115	−0.0599		−0.0599		
Sep 83	−0.0024	−0.0047		−0.0047		
Oct 83	0.0023	0.0326		0.0326		
Nov 83	−0.0231	−0.0537		−0.0537		
Dec 83	0.0403	0.0425		0.0425		
Jan 84	0.0077	0.0962		0.0962		
Feb 84	0.0199	0.0491		0.0491		
Mar 84	−0.0073	0.0148		0.0148		
Apr 84	−0.0268	−0.0380		−0.0380		
May 84	−0.0145	−0.0565		−0.0565		
Jun 84	0.0199	0.0193		0.0193		
Jul 84	0.0309	0.1049		0.1049		
Aug 84	0.0020	−0.0124		−0.0124		
Sep 84	0.0157	−0.0208		−0.0208		
Oct 84	−0.0055	−0.0301		−0.0301		
Nov 84	−0.0281	0.0086		0.0086		
Dec 84	0.0329	0.0608		0.0608		
Jan 85	0.0155	−0.0138		0.0300	0.1363	−0.0415
Feb 85	−0.0240	−0.0291		−0.0562	−0.0346	−0.0170
Mar 85	0.0403	−0.0134		−0.0026	−0.0059	−0.0184
Apr 85	0.0019	−0.0350		−0.0348	0.0224	−0.0388
May 85	0.0215	−0.0182		−0.0411	0.0915	−0.0153
Jun 85	−0.0083	−0.0088		0.0354	0.0116	−0.0332
Jul 85	0.0165	−0.0731		0.0113	−0.0241	−0.1236
Aug 85	−0.0417	0.0309		−0.0017	0.0800	0.0473
Sep 85	0.0795	0.0634		0.0146	0.0880	0.0907
Oct 85	0.0370	0.1112		0.0431	0.0343	0.1565
Nov 85	−0.0203	0.0777		0.1999	−0.0285	0.0240
Dec 85	−0.0179	0.1184		0.1592	0.0329	0.1005
Jan 86	0.0173	0.0570		0.0120	0.0697	0.0813
Feb 86	0.0534	0.1318		0.1685	0.3142	0.0940
Mar 86	−0.0253	0.0821		0.1741	0.1786	0.0055
Apr 86	−0.0226	−0.0253		−0.0500	0.0139	−0.0072
May 86	0.0702	0.1186		0.1865	0.0411	0.0687
Jun 86	0.0456	0.0342		0.0408	0.2589	0.0063

Table A.5.   (continued)

	Asia	East Asia	China	Korea	Philippines	Taiwan
Jul 86	0.0236	0.0588		0.1437	0.2378	−0.0457
Aug 86	0.0039	−0.0261		−0.0555	0.0480	−0.0030
Sep 86	0.0259	0.0552		−0.0162	0.3393	0.0888
Oct 86	0.0605	0.0148		−0.0422	0.0626	0.0638
Nov 86	−0.0390	0.0528		0.1023	0.0710	0.0030
Dec 86	0.0358	0.0375		−0.0025	0.1093	0.0636
Jan 87	0.0650	0.0501		0.0230	0.0991	0.0657
Feb 87	0.0799	0.0833		0.0389	0.0435	0.1330
Mar 87	0.0238	0.1088		0.1487	0.0583	0.0861
Apr 87	0.0951	0.1448		−0.1222	0.1186	0.3888
May 87	0.0351	0.0260		0.1012	0.0088	−0.0144
Jun 87	0.0013	0.0091		0.0285	0.4241	−0.0740
Jul 87	0.1266	0.1756		0.1644	0.1490	0.1906
Aug 87	0.0659	0.1231		−0.1053	−0.1218	0.3471
Sep 87	0.1455	0.3067		0.0222	−0.2398	0.5334
Oct 87	−0.2539	−0.2624		−0.0145	−0.0975	−0.3553
Nov 87	0.0150	0.0681		−0.0014	0.0086	0.1096
Dec 87	−0.0474	−0.1141		0.1279	0.1200	−0.2450
Jan 88	0.1158	0.1836		0.2097	−0.0004	0.1960
Feb 88	0.0923	0.1553		−0.0188	−0.0566	0.2365
Mar 88	0.0008	−0.0092		0.1098	0.0580	−0.0485
Apr 88	0.1493	0.1708		0.0261	0.0911	0.2271
May 88	0.0793	0.0779		0.0988	−0.0010	0.0761
Jun 88	0.0523	0.0495		0.0059	0.0890	0.0754
Jul 88	0.1419	0.1884		0.0387	0.0930	0.2851
Aug 88	0.0773	0.1275		−0.0984	−0.0199	0.2461
Sep 88	0.0357	0.0342		0.0326	−0.0348	0.0375
Oct 88	−0.1334	−0.1610		0.0955	0.0364	−0.2503
Nov 88	0.0913	0.1104		0.1400	0.0313	0.0983
Dec 88	−0.1005	−0.1214		0.1230	0.0563	−0.2498
Jan 89	0.1102	0.1204		−0.0206	0.0261	0.2308
Feb 89	0.0658	0.0870		0.0294	−0.0015	0.1243
Mar 89	0.0743	0.0823		0.0902	0.0785	0.0779
Apr 89	0.0312	0.0208		−0.0608	0.1721	0.0650
May 89	0.1396	0.1770		−0.0260	0.0726	0.2870
Jun 89	−0.0362	−0.0495		−0.0646	−0.0265	−0.0438
Jul 89	0.0285	0.0335		0.0574	0.2351	0.0190
Aug 89	0.0207	0.0222		0.0809	−0.0363	−0.0008
Sep 89	0.0177	0.0132		−0.0144	0.0551	0.0246
Oct 89	−0.0123	−0.0096		−0.0490	0.0616	0.0058
Nov 89	−0.0526	−0.0715		0.0112	0.0218	−0.1092
Dec 89	0.0570	0.0465		−0.0243	−0.1345	0.0867

Table A.5. (continued)

	Asia	East Asia	China	Korea	Philippines	Taiwan
Jan 90	0.1584	0.1994		−0.0325	−0.0467	0.3078
Feb 90	−0.0378	−0.0476		−0.0477	−0.0169	−0.0488
Mar 90	−0.0707	−0.0872		−0.0383	0.0460	−0.1110
Apr 90	−0.1343	−0.1510		−0.1928	−0.1156	−0.1356
May 90	−0.0692	−0.1078		0.1913	−0.1124	−0.2217
Jun 90	−0.1501	−0.1970		−0.1072	0.0719	−0.2644
Jul 90	0.0553	0.0297		−0.0472	0.0112	0.0859
Aug 90	−0.1983	−0.2531		−0.1196	−0.1878	−0.3414
Sep 90	−0.1234	−0.1343		0.0032	−0.2930	−0.2351
Oct 90	0.1032	0.1715		0.1459	−0.0328	0.2170
Nov 90	0.0743	0.1406		0.0091	0.0168	0.2851
Dec 90	0.0304	0.0311		0.0006	0.0305	0.0559
Jan 91	−0.0770	−0.1040		−0.0746	0.0566	−0.1369
Feb 91	0.1481	0.1597		0.0604	0.2718	0.2399
Mar 91	0.0013	−0.0121		−0.0467	0.1173	0.0055
Apr 91	0.0540	0.0787		−0.0210	0.0039	0.1555
May 91	−0.0255	−0.0418		−0.0440	0.0765	−0.0479
Jun 91	−0.0118	0.0052		−0.0119	−0.0708	0.0211
Jul 91	0.0075	0.0120		0.2112	−0.0291	−0.1036
Aug 91	−0.0631	−0.0758		−0.0385	−0.0013	−0.1111
Sep 91	0.0224	0.0488		0.0296	−0.0938	0.0770
Oct 91	−0.0461	−0.0647		−0.0425	0.0621	−0.0919
Nov 91	−0.0097	−0.0304		−0.0747	0.0690	0.0011
Dec 91	0.0215	0.0007		−0.0678	0.0548	0.0528
Jan 92	0.1241	0.1408		0.1006	0.1166	0.1748
Feb 92	−0.0200	−0.0803		−0.1275	−0.0211	−0.0505
Mar 92	−0.0055	−0.0762		−0.0632	−0.0207	−0.0894
Apr 92	−0.0320	−0.0254		0.0091	0.0839	−0.0590
May 92	−0.0501	−0.0299		−0.1079	0.1039	0.0146
Jun 92	0.0242	0.0117		−0.0043	0.1501	0.0069
Jul 92	−0.0622	−0.0849		−0.0660	−0.0143	−0.1061
Aug 92	0.0020	0.0036		0.0960	−0.0134	−0.0563
Sep 92	−0.0053	−0.0749		−0.0769	−0.0436	−0.0779
Oct 92	0.0752	0.1167		0.2649	−0.0146	0.0204
Nov 92	0.0042	0.0452		0.0978	−0.0865	0.0130
Dec 92	−0.0233	−0.0348		−0.0048	−0.0404	−0.0660
Jan 93	0.0166	0.0092	0.3251	−0.0433	0.0735	−0.0037
Feb 93	0.0677	0.1399	0.1702	−0.0499	0.1104	0.3454
Mar 93	−0.0067	0.0286	−0.2299	0.0605	−0.0273	0.0724
Apr 93	0.0447	0.0343	0.2897	0.0828	0.0574	−0.0545
May 93	−0.0102	−0.0432	−0.2300	0.0265	−0.0234	−0.0578
Jun 93	−0.0290	−0.0616	−0.2330	−0.0215	−0.0199	−0.0682

Table A.5. (continued)

	Asia	East Asia	China	Korea	Philippines	Taiwan
Jul 93	0.0210	−0.0158	0.1508	−0.0380	0.0855	−0.0393
Aug 93	0.0207	−0.0360	−0.0291	−0.0662	0.0089	−0.0143
Sep 93	0.0294	0.0188	−0.0103	0.0704	0.0953	−0.0375
Oct 93	0.1006	0.0538	−0.0615	0.0217	0.1738	0.0934
Nov 93	0.0633	0.0680	0.1157	0.0714	0.0476	0.0588
Dec 93	0.2239	0.2630	−0.1036	0.1052	0.3768	0.4967
Jan 94	−0.0175	0.0350	−0.1238	0.1322	−0.0918	0.0103
Feb 94	−0.0276	−0.0644	−0.0045	−0.0145	−0.0280	−0.1259
Mar 94	−0.0940	−0.0581	−0.1316	−0.0802	−0.0408	−0.0230
Apr 94	0.0537	0.0639	−0.1461	0.0677	0.0512	0.1060
May 94	0.0162	0.0207	−0.0754	0.0336	0.1036	0.0089
Jun 94	−0.0060	−0.0115	−0.1504	−0.0103	−0.0781	0.0210
Jul 94	0.0492	0.0585	−0.2037	−0.0128	0.0504	0.1544
Aug 94	0.0941	0.0838	0.9968	0.0358	0.0981	0.0436
Sep 94	0.0251	0.0663	0.0492	0.1390	−0.0377	0.0321
Oct 94	−0.0203	−0.0395	−0.1818	0.0166	0.0652	−0.0840
Nov 94	−0.0584	−0.0344	0.0220	−0.0378	−0.0749	−0.0299
Dec 94	0.0010	0.0306	−0.0596	−0.0550	0.0080	0.1315
Jan 95	−0.1030	−0.1094	−0.1246	−0.0932	−0.1265	−0.1173
Feb 95	0.0334	0.0005	−0.0074	−0.0299	−0.0040	0.0283
Mar 95	0.0065	0.0363	0.1416	0.0836	−0.0524	0.0000
Apr 95	−0.0349	−0.0526	−0.1005	−0.0028	0.0179	−0.1006
May 95	0.0645	0.0170	0.1708	−0.0040	0.1318	−0.0195
Jun 95	−0.0155	−0.0232	−0.0835	0.0096	0.0069	−0.0494

Note: Blanks in columns indicate market was not yet covered by the EMDB.

Table A.6. Asia and South Asia: Total Value-Weighted Stock Returns, January 1976–June 1995

	Asia	South Asia	India	Indonesia	Malaysia	Pakistan	Sri Lanka	Thailand
Jan 76	0.1683	0.1247	0.1829					−0.0146
Feb 76	−0.0039	−0.0078	−0.0143					0.0111
Mar 76	0.0027	−0.0253	−0.0197					−0.0410
Apr 76	−0.0053	−0.0076	−0.0329					0.0656
May 76	−0.0448	−0.0483	−0.0486					−0.0475
Jun 76	0.0614	0.0633	0.0922					−0.0109
Jul 76	0.0316	0.0508	0.0642					0.0140
Aug 76	0.0203	0.0517	0.0537					0.0457
Sep 76	0.0282	0.0367	0.0417					0.0220
Oct 76	0.0067	−0.0298	−0.0481					0.0274
Nov 76	−0.0005	−0.0210	−0.0223					−0.0173
Dec 76	0.0729	0.0408	0.0432					0.0343
Jan 77	0.0528	0.0155	0.0001					0.0576
Feb 77	0.0322	0.0210	0.0145					0.0377
Mar 77	0.0345	0.0605	0.0366					0.1207
Apr 77	−0.0105	0.0198	0.0014					0.0637
May 77	0.0335	0.0240	0.0206					0.0318
Jun 77	0.0205	0.0055	−0.0347					0.0954
Jul 77	0.0121	0.0299	−0.0035					0.0957
Aug 77	0.0966	0.1208	0.0486					0.2486
Sep 77	0.0688	−0.0210	−0.0297					−0.0083
Oct 77	0.0994	0.1155	0.0042					0.2767
Nov 77	−0.0490	−0.0684	−0.0630					−0.0745
Dec 77	0.0868	0.0658	0.1228					0.0038
Jan 78	0.0935	0.0649	0.0531					0.0788
Feb 78	0.0247	0.0027	0.0084					−0.0038
Mar 78	0.0076	0.0135	0.0734					−0.0565
Apr 78	0.0161	−0.0086	0.0019					−0.0223
May 78	0.0405	0.0263	0.0464					−0.0004
Jun 78	0.0348	0.0166	0.0199					0.0120
Jul 78	0.0303	0.0064	0.0316					−0.0285
Aug 78	0.0260	0.0226	0.0047					0.0483
Sep 78	0.0056	0.0715	0.0707					0.0725
Oct 78	0.0023	0.1282	0.0734					0.1973
Nov 78	−0.0261	−0.0772	−0.0961					−0.0567
Dec 78	0.0441	0.0317	0.0495					0.0139
Jan 79	−0.0491	−0.0337	0.0131					−0.0762
Feb 79	−0.0430	−0.0301	0.0201					−0.0798
Mar 79	−0.0254	0.0260	0.0686					−0.0203
Apr 79	−0.0728	−0.0530	0.0164					−0.1376
May 79	−0.0152	0.0155	−0.0153					0.0599
Jun 79	−0.0010	0.0118	0.0535					−0.0437

108

Table A.6.   (continued)

	Asia	South Asia	India	Indonesia	Malaysia	Pakistan	Sri Lanka	Thailand
Jul 79	−0.0221	−0.0138	−0.0261					0.0041
Aug 79	0.1554	−0.0238	−0.0218					−0.0267
Sep 79	0.0182	0.0291	0.0202					0.0416
Oct 79	−0.0963	−0.0363	−0.0180					−0.0617
Nov 79	0.0424	−0.0179	−0.0193					−0.0159
Dec 79	−0.0355	0.0410	0.0751					−0.0090
Jan 80	−0.0535	−0.0190	0.0280					−0.0938
Feb 80	−0.0003	0.0401	0.0534					0.0160
Mar 80	−0.0055	−0.0116	−0.0305					0.0241
Apr 80	0.0897	0.0075	0.0183					−0.0120
May 80	−0.0038	−0.0106	0.0055					−0.0415
Jun 80	−0.0164	0.0395	0.0306					0.0574
Jul 80	−0.0012	0.0262	0.0462					−0.0130
Aug 80	−0.0040	0.0261	0.0759					−0.0770
Sep 80	−0.0433	−0.0116	−0.0186					0.0052
Oct 80	−0.061	−0.0051	−0.0055					−0.0041
Nov 80	0.0645	0.0877	0.0782					0.1101
Dec 80	−0.0036	0.0246	0.0454					−0.0227
Jan 81	0.0551	−0.0273	−0.0468					0.0194
Feb 81	0.0065	0.0536	0.0753					0.0047
Mar 81	0.0664	0.0720	0.0976					0.0102
Apr 81	0.0809	0.0342	0.0510					−0.0104
May 81	−0.0251	−0.0628	−0.0649					−0.0567
Jun 81	0.1753	0.1037	0.1615					−0.0599
Jul 81	−0.0609	−0.0444	−0.0319					−0.0890
Aug 81	−0.0658	−0.0701	−0.0736					−0.0573
Sep 81	−0.0253	0.0182	0.0115					0.0430
Oct 81	−0.0277	0.0207	0.0243					0.0077
Nov 81	0.0598	0.0359	0.0355					0.0373
Dec 81	−0.0050	0.0362	0.0480					−0.0089
Jan 82	0.0104	−0.0294	−0.0340					−0.0111
Feb 82	0.0218	0.0125	0.0192					−0.0137
Mar 82	−0.0306	−0.0402	−0.0532					0.0071
Apr 82	−0.0023	0.0442	0.0512					0.0193
May 82	−0.0235	0.0159	0.0155					0.0175
Jun 82	−0.0056	−0.0649	−0.0857					0.0097
Jul 82	0.0011	0.0118	0.0116					0.0127
Aug 82	−0.0209	−0.0063	−0.0229					0.0469
Sep 82	0.0492	0.0898	0.0548					0.1965
Oct 82	−0.0171	−0.0366	−0.0475					−0.0062
Nov 82	0.0172	0.0248	0.0299					0.0113
Dec 82	0.0446	0.0328	0.0490					−0.0111

Table A.6. (continued)

	Asia	South Asia	India	Indonesia	Malaysia	Pakistan	Sri Lanka	Thailand
Jan 83	−0.0518	−0.0620	−0.0929					0.0268
Feb 83	0.0270	0.0256	0.0223					0.0340
Mar 83	−0.0376	−0.0372	−0.0540					0.0061
Apr 83	0.0626	0.0235	0.0044					0.0700
May 83	0.0420	0.0906	0.1133					0.0391
Jun 83	−0.0173	−0.0047	−0.0050					−0.0040
Jul 83	0.0064	0.0090	0.0002					0.0300
Aug 83	−0.0115	0.0109	−0.0009					0.0380
Sep 83	−0.0024	−0.0014	−0.0010					−0.0024
Oct 83	0.0023	−0.0112	−0.0043					−0.0275
Nov 83	−0.0231	−0.0086	−0.0040					−0.0200
Dec 83	0.0403	0.0393	0.0505					0.0117
Jan 84	0.0077	−0.0322	−0.0398					−0.0137
Feb 84	0.0199	0.0062	0.0140					−0.0135
Mar 84	−0.0073	−0.0177	−0.0214					−0.0093
Apr 84	−0.0268	−0.0213	−0.0471					0.0379
May 84	−0.0145	0.0058	0.0115					−0.0061
Jun 84	0.0199	0.0201	0.0261					0.0071
Jul 84	0.0309	−0.0053	−0.0053					−0.0053
Aug 84	0.0020	0.0098	−0.0093					0.0512
Sep 84	0.0157	0.0355	0.0496					0.0059
Oct 84	−0.0055	0.0073	−0.0058					0.0363
Nov 84	−0.0281	−0.0465	−0.0217					−0.0988
Dec 84	0.0329	0.0181	0.0252					0.0018
Jan 85	0.0155	0.0275	0.0418		0.0324	0.0069		−0.0328
Feb 85	−0.0240	−0.0221	0.0094		−0.0301	−0.0223		−0.0020
Mar 85	0.0403	0.0601	0.1986		0.0301	0.0352		0.0948
Apr 85	0.0019	0.0145	0.1081		−0.0152	0.0465		0.0740
May 85	0.0215	0.0344	0.0308		0.0376	0.0511		0.0067
Jun 85	−0.0083	−0.0081	0.2043		−0.0649	−0.0100		0.0004
Jul 85	0.0165	0.0452	0.1565		0.0094	−0.0028		0.0511
Aug 85	−0.0417	−0.0623	−0.0897		−0.0560	−0.0082		−0.0507
Sep 85	0.0795	0.0845	−0.0531		0.1534	−0.0168		−0.0047
Oct 85	0.0370	0.0143	0.0988		−0.0108	0.0516		−0.0133
Nov 85	−0.0203	−0.0530	0.0309		−0.0903	0.0497		−0.0250
Dec 85	−0.0179	−0.0701	0.0479		−0.1184	−0.0018		−0.0874
Jan 86	0.0173	0.0003	0.1353		−0.0660	0.0038		0.0488
Feb 86	0.0534	0.0142	0.1309		−0.0522	0.0406		0.0231
Mar 86	−0.0253	−0.0850	−0.1503		−0.0510	−0.0156		−0.0634
Apr 86	−0.0226	−0.0209	0.0558		−0.0765	0.0526		0.0155
May 86	0.0702	0.0440	0.0346		0.0712	−0.0505		−0.0113
Jun 86	0.0456	0.0523	−0.0041		0.1221	−0.0399		0.0310

Table A.6. (continued)

	Asia	South Asia	India	Indonesia	Malaysia	Pakistan	Sri Lanka	Thailand
Jul 86	0.0236	0.0034	−0.0045		−0.0080	0.0545		0.1230
Aug 86	0.0039	0.0220	−0.0750		0.1083	−0.0086		0.0740
Sep 86	0.0259	0.0090	0.0601		−0.0498	0.0809		0.1049
Oct 86	0.0605	0.0885	−0.0461		0.2083	−0.0086		0.1279
Nov 86	−0.0390	−0.0916	−0.1611		−0.0648	0.0294		0.0049
Dec 86	0.0358	0.0346	0.0472		0.0108	0.0710		0.1162
Jan 87	0.0650	0.0755	0.0468		0.1104	0.0268		−0.0060
Feb 87	0.0799	0.0775	−0.0025		0.1387	0.0088		−0.0114
Mar 87	0.0238	−0.0330	−0.0680		−0.0371	−0.0263		0.1069
Apr 87	0.0951	0.0572	−0.0430		0.1001	−0.0176		0.0935
May 87	0.0351	0.0427	−0.0505		0.0819	0.0202		0.0323
Jun 87	0.0013	−0.0050	−0.0917		0.0086	−0.0168		0.0994
Jul 87	0.1266	0.0863	0.0777		0.1024	−0.0194		0.0390
Aug 87	0.0659	0.0147	0.0353		−0.0137	0.0192		0.1401
Sep 87	0.1455	−0.0158	−0.0767		−0.0478	0.0346		0.2301
Oct 87	−0.2539	−0.2426	0.0104		−0.3059	−0.0030		−0.3383
Nov 87	0.0150	−0.0530	−0.0181		−0.0939	0.0056		0.0337
Dec 87	−0.0474	0.0434	0.0311		0.0601	0.0401		0.0110
Jan 88	0.1158	0.0423	−0.0153		0.0484	0.0569		0.1419
Feb 88	0.0923	−0.0192	−0.0589		−0.0497	0.0179		0.1505
Mar 88	0.0008	0.0218	−0.0440		0.0545	0.0302		0.0240
Apr 88	0.1493	0.1054	0.1717		0.0780	0.0063		0.1170
May 88	0.0793	0.0822	0.2376		0.0355	0.0129		−0.0016
Jun 88	0.0523	0.0598	−0.0301		0.1203	−0.0252		0.0625
Jul 88	0.1419	0.0192	0.0491		0.0031	0.0314		0.0180
Aug 88	0.0773	−0.0713	−0.0392		−0.1024	−0.0169		−0.0452
Sep 88	0.0357	0.0420	0.1150		0.0120	−0.0174		0.0207
Oct 88	−0.1334	0.0058	−0.0426		0.0429	−0.0015		−0.0426
Nov 88	0.0913	0.0109	0.0874		−0.0014	−0.0095		−0.0601
Dec 88	−0.1005	−0.0027	−0.0582		0.0235	0.0455		−0.0116
Jan 89	0.1102	0.0682	0.0093		0.0841	0.0147		0.1134
Feb 89	0.0658	−0.0146	−0.0422		−0.0047	0.0236		−0.0007
Mar 89	0.0743	0.0410	0.0597		0.0403	0.0715		0.0068
Apr 89	0.0312	0.0767	0.0461		0.0843	−0.0316		0.1228
May 89	0.1396	−0.0160	−0.1411		0.0249	−0.0516		0.0773
Jun 89	−0.0362	0.0306	0.1124		−0.0193	0.0277		0.0642
Jul 89	0.0285	0.0049	−0.0812		0.0503	0.0003		0.0062
Aug 89	0.0207	0.0132	0.0222		−0.0154	0.0149		0.0829
Sep 89	0.0177	0.0397	0.0167		0.0573	0.0052		0.0251
Oct 89	−0.0123	−0.0254	−0.0039		−0.0517	−0.0257		0.0188
Nov 89	−0.0526	0.0387	−0.0544		0.0505	−0.0065		0.1236
Dec 89	0.0570	0.1022	0.1317		0.1005	0.0365		0.0816

Table A.6. (continued)

	Asia	South Asia	India	Indonesia	Malaysia	Pakistan	Sri Lanka	Thailand
Jan 90	0.1584	−0.0197	−0.1028	0.1182	0.0222	0.0208		−0.0393
Feb 90	−0.0378	0.0211	−0.0201	0.1336	0.0691	−0.0021		−0.0552
Mar 90	−0.0707	0.0202	0.1152	0.1874	−0.0485	0.0146		0.0295
Apr 90	−0.1343	−0.0526	−0.0018	−0.0314	−0.1104	−0.0344		0.0007
May 90	−0.0692	0.0953	0.0185	−0.0071	0.1301	−0.0225		0.1659
Jun 90	−0.1501	0.0101	0.0453	−0.0342	−0.0149	0.0331		0.0386
Jul 90	0.0553	0.1244	0.2629	0.0040	0.0875	0.0345		0.1118
Aug 90	−0.1983	−0.0642	0.1475	−0.0507	−0.1374	−0.0009		−0.1729
Sep 90	−0.1234	−0.1023	0.0596	−0.1973	−0.1462	0.0091		−0.2251
Oct 90	0.1032	−0.0250	−0.0905	−0.1026	0.0530	0.0388		−0.0123
Nov 90	0.0743	−0.0731	−0.0895	−0.0556	−0.0483	0.0048		−0.1090
Dec 90	0.0304	0.0285	−0.1040	0.0843	0.0917	0.0000		0.1100
Jan 91	−0.0770	−0.0129	−0.0776	−0.0837	−0.0159	−0.0036		0.0948
Feb 91	0.1481	0.1231	0.1694	0.0260	0.1137	−0.0137		0.1466
Mar 91	0.0013	0.0304	−0.0514	0.0301	0.0367	0.0285		0.0968
Apr 91	0.0540	0.0021	0.0110	0.0119	0.0058	0.0797		−0.0208
May 91	−0.0255	0.0089	0.0187	−0.0436	0.0641	0.0245		−0.0910
Jun 91	−0.0118	−0.0456	−0.0514	−0.1169	−0.0296	0.0700		−0.0592
Jul 91	0.0075	−0.0019	0.0376	0.0016	−0.0185	0.1966		−0.0214
Aug 91	−0.0631	−0.0365	0.0759	−0.1300	−0.0704	−0.0031		−0.0325
Sep 91	0.0224	−0.0309	0.0562	−0.2088	−0.0396	0.0190		−0.0415
Oct 91	−0.0461	−0.0055	−0.0014	−0.0989	0.0204	0.0539		−0.0458
Nov 91	−0.0097	0.0329	0.0123	0.0753	0.0017	0.3523		0.0707
Dec 91	0.0215	0.0614	−0.0090	0.0469	0.0572	0.3147		0.1087
Jan 92	0.1241	0.0942	0.2070	0.1426	0.0573	−0.1340		0.0951
Feb 92	−0.0200	0.0899	0.2483	−0.0103	0.0774	−0.1017		0.0229
Mar 92	−0.0055	0.1031	0.3526	−0.0089	−0.0103	0.0057		0.0612
Apr 92	−0.0320	−0.0406	−0.1121	0.0001	0.0209	0.1649		−0.0787
May 92	−0.0501	−0.0767	−0.2438	0.0880	0.0056	0.0552		−0.0645
Jun 92	0.0242	0.0413	0.0295	0.0460	0.0179	0.0633		0.0982
Jul 92	−0.0622	−0.0322	−0.0964	−0.0024	0.0163	−0.1585		−0.0355
Aug 92	0.0020	0.0001	0.0963	−0.0705	−0.0380	−0.0864		0.0159
Sep 92	−0.0053	0.0811	0.0956	−0.0204	0.0646	0.0757		0.1391
Oct 92	0.0752	0.0317	−0.1269	0.0264	0.0802	0.0411		0.1364
Nov 92	0.0042	−0.0419	−0.0978	−0.0811	0.0098	−0.0774		−0.0594
Dec 92	−0.0233	−0.0091	0.0227	−0.0627	−0.0419	0.0041		0.0393
Jan 93	0.0166	0.0264	0.0270	0.0418	−0.0318	0.0003	−0.0948	0.1280
Feb 93	0.0677	−0.0080	−0.0657	0.0886	0.0295	−0.0611	0.0067	−0.0298
Mar 93	−0.0067	−0.0496	−0.1780	0.0234	0.0198	−0.0315	0.0130	−0.0755
Apr 93	0.0447	0.0585	−0.0621	0.0159	0.1420	−0.0236	−0.0420	0.0214
May 93	−0.0102	0.0328	0.0638	0.0973	0.0425	0.0523	0.0529	−0.0287
Jun 93	−0.0290	0.0101	0.0195	0.0574	−0.0314	0.0990	0.1058	0.0668

Table A.6. (continued)

	Asia	South Asia	India	Indonesia	Malaysia	Pakistan	Sri Lanka	Thailand
Jul 93	0.0210	0.0621	0.0689	−0.0084	0.0728	−0.0120	0.1584	0.0641
Aug 93	0.0207	0.0798	0.1320	0.1947	0.0786	−0.0552	−0.0428	0.0303
Sep 93	0.0294	0.0393	0.0423	−0.0183	0.0578	0.0442	0.0022	0.0164
Oct 93	0.1006	0.1435	−0.0178	0.0777	0.1366	0.1376	0.1216	0.3218
Nov 93	0.0633	0.0593	0.2049	0.0139	0.0270	0.1062	0.1684	0.0295
Dec 93	0.2239	0.1902	0.0649	0.1380	0.2088	0.2603	0.0317	0.2622
Jan 94	−0.0175	−0.0651	0.1722	0.0279	−0.1517	0.0253	0.1562	−0.1023
Feb 94	−0.0276	0.0068	0.0455	−0.1137	0.0558	0.0857	0.2156	−0.0896
Mar 94	−0.0940	−0.1252	−0.1276	−0.1215	−0.1521	0.0066	−0.1387	−0.0882
Apr 94	0.0537	0.0441	−0.0285	−0.0484	0.1039	−0.0591	−0.1326	0.0494
May 94	0.0162	0.0118	0.0202	0.1320	−0.0391	−0.0709	−0.0244	0.0847
Jun 94	−0.0060	−0.0009	0.0605	−0.0851	0.0101	0.0589	−0.0057	−0.0524
Jul 94	0.0492	0.0405	0.0237	−0.0193	0.0323	−0.0139	0.0017	0.0960
Aug 94	0.0941	0.1040	0.0749	0.1457	0.1075	−0.0208	0.0549	0.1273
Sep 94	0.0251	−0.0138	−0.0495	−0.0257	0.0041	0.0296	0.0997	−0.0168
Oct 94	−0.0203	−0.0003	−0.0289	0.0484	−0.0179	−0.0237	−0.0429	0.0427
Nov 94	−0.0584	−0.0827	−0.0199	−0.1022	−0.0875	−0.0469	−0.0310	−0.1214
Dec 94	0.0010	−0.0301	−0.0478	−0.0104	−0.0377	−0.0387	−0.0916	−0.0058
Jan 95	−0.1030	−0.0959	−0.0757	−0.0720	−0.1096	−0.1095	−0.0501	−0.0971
Feb 95	0.0334	0.0665	−0.0550	0.0774	0.1405	0.0454	−0.1631	0.0751
Mar 95	0.0065	−0.0215	−0.0290	−0.0719	0.0058	−0.1100	0.0799	−0.0364
Apr 95	−0.0349	−0.0172	−0.0430	−0.0393	−0.0164	−0.0275	−0.1278	0.0101
May 95	0.0645	0.1103	0.0470	0.1895	0.1208	−0.0417	−0.0420	0.1383
Jun 95	−0.0155	−0.0088	−0.0352	0.0524	−0.0171	0.0757	0.0275	0.0004

Note: Blanks in columns indicate market was not yet covered by the EMDB.

References and Selected Bibliography

AIMR. 1997. *Implementing Global Equity Strategy: Spotlight on Asia* (Charlottesville, VA: Association for Investment Management and Research).

———. 1996. *Investing Worldwide VII: Focus on Emerging Markets* (Charlottesville, VA: Association for Investment Management and Research).

———. Forthcoming 1997. *Investing Worldwide VIII: Developments in Global Portfolio Management* (Charlottesville, VA: Association for Investment Management and Research).

Bailey, Warren, and Y. Peter Chung. 1995. "Exchange Rate Fluctuations, Political Risk, and Stock Returns: Some Evidence from an Emerging Market." *Journal of Financial and Quantitative Analysis*, vol. 30, no. 4:541–61.

Barry, C.B., and L.J. Lockwood. 1995. "New Directions in Research on Emerging Capital Markets." *Financial Markets, Institutions, and Instruments*, vol. 4, no. 5:15–36.

Barry, C.B., and M. Rodriguez. 1997. "Risk, Return, and Performance of Latin America's Equity Markets, 1975–95." Working paper, Texas Christian University.

Barry, C.B., J.W. Peavy III, and M. Rodriguez. 1997a. "A Convenient Way to Invest in the Emerging Markets." *Emerging Markets Quarterly*, vol. 1, no. 1:41–48.

———. 1997b. "The Performance Characteristics of Emerging Capital Markets." Working paper, Texas Christian University.

Bekaert, G. 1995. "Market Integration and Investment Barriers in Emerging Equity Markets." *World Bank Economic Review*, vol. 9, no. 9:75–107.

Bekaert, G., and C.R. Harvey. 1995. "Time-Varying World Market Integration." *Journal of Finance*, vol. 50, no. 2:403–43.

Bekaert, G., and M. Urias. 1996. "Diversification, Integration, and Emerging Market Closed End Funds." *Journal of Finance*, vol. 51, no. 3:835–69.

Claessens, Stijn, Susmita Dasgupta, and Jack Glen. 1995. "Return Behavior in Emerging Stock Markets." *World Bank Economic Review*, vol. 9, no. 1:131–51.

Divecha, A.B., J. Drach, and D. Stefek. 1992. "Emerging Markets: A Quantitative Perspective." *Journal of Portfolio Management*, vol. 19, no. 1:41–56.

Edwards, S. 1995. *Crisis and Reform in Latin America: From Despair to Hope*. New York: Oxford University Press.

Frankel, J., and S. Schmulker. 1996. "Crisis, Contagion, and Country Funds: Effects on East Asia and Latin America." Working Paper No. PB96–04, Federal Reserve Bank of San Francisco.

Goetzmann, W.N., and P. Jorion. 1996a. "Re-emerging Markets." Working paper, Yale School of Management.

———. 1996b. "A Century of Global Stock Markets." Working paper, Yale School of Management.

Harvey, C.R. 1994. "Portfolio Enhancement Using Emerging Markets and Conditioning Information." In *Portfolio Investment in Developing Countries*. Stijn Claessens and Shan Gooptu, eds. The World Bank Discussion Series, Washington DC:110–44.

IFC. 1995a. *Emerging Stock Markets Factbook* (Washington DC: International Finance Corporation).

IFC. 1995b. *Emerging Market Factbook 1995* (Washington DC: International Finance Corporation).

IFC.1993. *IFC Index Methodology* (Washington DC: International Finance Corporation).

Karnosky, Denis S., and Brian D. Singer. 1994. *Global Asset Management and Performance Attribution*. Charlottesville, VA: Research Foundation of the Institute of Chartered Financial Analysts.

Price, M.P. 1994. *Emerging Stock Markets*. New York: McGraw-Hill.

Sachs, J., A. Tornell, and A. Velasco. 1996. "Financial Crises in Emerging Markets: The Lessons from 1995." Working Paper 5576. Cambridge, MA: National Bureau of Economic Research.

Stanley, M.T. 1995. *Guide to Investing in Emerging Markets*. Chicago: Richard D. Irwin Publishing.

Selected Publications

AIMR

Economic Analysis for Investment Professionals, 1997

Finding Reality in Reported Earnings, 1997
Jan R. Squires, CFA, *Editor*

Global Equity Investing, 1996

Global Portfolio Management, 1996
Jan R. Squires, CFA, *Editor*

Implementing Global Equity Strategy: Spotlight on Asia, 1997

Investing in Small-Cap and Microcap Securities, 1997

Managing Endowment and Foundation Funds, 1996

Managing Investment Firms: People and Culture, 1996
Jan R. Squires, CFA, *Editor*

The Media Industry, 1996

Merck & Company: A Comprehensive Equity Valuation Analysis, 1996
Randall S. Billingsley, CFA

Risk Management, 1996

Standards of Practice Casebook, 1996

Standards of Practice Handbook, 7th edition, 1996

AIMR Performance Presentation Standards Handbook, 2nd edition, 1997

Research Foundation

Company Performance and Measures of Value Added, 1996
by Pamela P. Peterson, CFA, and David R. Peterson

Currency Management: Concepts and Practices, 1996
by Roger G. Clarke and Mark P. Kritzman, CFA

Information Trading, Volatility, and Liquidity in Option Markets, 1997
by Joseph A. Cherian and Anne Fremault Vila

Initial Dividends and Implications for Investors, 1997
by James W. Wansley, CFA, William R. Lane, CFA, and Phillip R. Daves

Interest Rate and Currency Swaps: A Tutorial, 1995
by Keith C. Brown, CFA, and Donald J. Smith

Interest Rate Modeling and the Risk Premiums in Interest Rate Swaps, 1997
Robert Brooks, CFA